FLYING BOATS OF THE SOLENT

FLYING BOATS
OF THE
SOLENT

NORMAN HULL

·AVIATION HERITAGE·
from
The NOSTALGIA Collection

Anthony Kitcher

Dedicated to the memory of

Angela Kitcher

whose career as an Air Hostess was tragically ended
at 22.55 hours on 15 November 1957 when Aquila Airways
'Solent' flying boat registration G-AKNU *Sydney* crashed
on the Isle of Wight.

A Silver Link book
from
The NOSTALGIA *Collection*

© Norman Hull 2002

*All rights reserved. No part of this
publication may be reproduced, stored in
a retrieval system or transmitted, in any
form or by any means, electronic,
mechanical, photocopying, recording or
otherwise, without prior permission in
writing from Silver Link Publishing Ltd.*

First published in 2002

British Library Cataloguing in
Publication Data

A catalogue record for this book is
available from the British Library.

ISBN 1 85794 161 6

Silver Link Publishing Ltd
The Trundle
Ringstead Road
Great Addington
Kettering
Northants NN14 4BW

Tel/Fax: 01536 330588
email: sales@nostalgiacollection.com
Website:
www.nostalgiacollection.com

Printed and bound in Great Britain

All photographs and items of
ephemera not otherwise credited are
from the author's collection.

**Frontispiece A BOAC flying boat
over Cunard's *Queen Elizabeth*
long before aircraft carried more
passengers than the once elegant
'greyhounds' of the North Atlantic.**
From a painting by Ivan Berryman

CONTENTS

ACKNOWLEDGEMENTS

My sincerest thanks go to the following commercial sources, individuals and organisations that have supplied photographic and other material. I am also grateful for the moral and practical support that I received when eye problems made life somewhat difficult.

Commercial organisations
Bournemouth Daily Echo, Cobham plc, Thomas Cook, Foynes Flying Boat Museum, GKN Westland Aerospace, Hampshire Fire & Rescue, Madeira Tourist Board, MAP of Aslackby, Adrian Meredith/BOAC, Reed Travel Group (Roger Cooper), Southampton Aviation Museum, *Southern Evening Echo*, and Vickers plc.

Individuals
Special thanks go to John Hankin for his Foreword, and to Huw Thomas and Alan Dunkley for their proof-reading.

Numerous other people have helped me in one way or another, especially Barbara, my wife, and other members of my family who all had to cope with my eye problems as well as flying boats.

The following deserve recognition: the late George Barnes, Ivan Berryman, Christopher Blackburn, Dave Blake, Joao Borges (Madeira), A. Breese, Doris Brinkley, Ken Carmichael, Brian Cassidy, Stephen J. Dyer, Dave Etheridge, Mrs B. Evans, John Evans, Vic Hodgkinson, Margaret Haynes, Michael and Tina Hull, Margaret Johnson, Tony Kitcher, James Labouchere, Mary Lobley, Mrs McCorry (via John Evans), Reg Oliver, Vic Pitt, Lola Soutter, Gillian Spencer, Noel Tatt, Deborah Thomas, Don Townend, Peter Townsend, and Colin Van Geffen.

BIBLIOGRAPHY

Cassidy, Brian *Flying Empires* (1996)
City of Southampton, tribute by *Spitfire – 60th Anniversary*
Coster, Graham *Corsairville* (2000)
Cruddas, Colin *In Cobham's Company* (1994)
Davies, Ken *New Forest Airfields* (1992)
Evans, John *The Sunderland Flying Boat Queen*, Vols 1 & 2 (1987 & 1993)
Hannah, Donald *Shorts Fly Past Reference Library* (1987)
Hilliker, Ivor J. *A Solent Flight* (1990)
Hooks, Mike *Shorts Aircraft* (1995)
Hughes, Mike *The Hebrides At War* (2001)
Hull, Norman *Eagles Over Water* (1994)
Kemp, Anthony *Southampton at War* (Southern Daily Echo, 1994)
Mondey, David *The Schneider Trophy* (1975)
Moody, Bert *150 Years of Southampton Docks* (1988)
Pannell, J. P. M. *Old Southampton Shores* (1967)
Powell, Air Commodore 'Taffy' *Ferryman* (1982)
Rance, Adrian B. *Sea Planes and Flying Boats of The Solent* (1981)
Sims, Philip E. *Adventurous Empires* (2000)
Tagg, A. E. and Wheeler R. L. *From Sea to Air* (1989)
Taylor, John W. R. *Aircraft* (1971)
Wheeler, Ray L. *Saunders Roe* (1998)
Williams, David L. *Wings Over The Island* (c1998)
Woods, Eric (Timber) *From Flying Boats to Flying Jets* (1997)

Various aviation magazines, videos, audio tapes, and Southampton Town and City guidebooks

FOREWORD

by
John Hankin
Station Manager, Aquila Airways, Southampton, 1949-57

As someone who was fortunate enough to be involved with Aquila in the post-Second World War years, I was pleased to be asked to provide the Foreword to this fascinating history of flying boats over its operating life.

The book reflects the vital role played by the individuals and persons associated with this importunate industry – an industry that has provided an integral contribution to this nation's history.

I am sure that readers will derive the same pleasure that I did.

Embarkation for the proving flight to Capri on Friday 21 May 1954: Aquila founder Barry Aikman escorts Gracie Fields towards the pontoon at Southampton, followed by John Hankin (in uniform) with Miss Fields's husband Boris Alpervici. *Dave Blake*

A letter received from actress Constance Cumming, who was a passenger on the first flight to Madeira in 1949. Her words are captured in the photograph of swans with Imperial Airways' RMA (Royal Mail Airliner) *Ceres*. *Author's collection/Alan Breese*

Dear Dr Hull,

Indeed I do remember the flight to Madeira – it was the first time I had ever landed on water in a plane – and I thought it was magical –

I have no Baggage Ticket or anything of that nature, I am sorry, as a momento –

But I shall never forget the visit in Madeira – such a beautiful country with the hills and gardens. Beautiful flowers everywhere – but most of all gliding down onto the clear water of the Harbour like a swan – what an entrance!

My best wishes to you and many Thanks – Sincerely Constance Cummings

INTRODUCTION

The challenge to condense the maritime aviation heritage of Southern Hampshire and the Isle of Wight into one book has been a daunting task. However, by separating the narrative from the 'nuts and bolts' detail, it is hoped that it will appeal to more people than just 'flying boat nutters' like myself.

The period covered by this book is nearly 100 years and includes about 11 years of hostility when this country was at war against Germany and Japan. During that time many different types of marine aircraft were designed and built, such as the Sopwith 'Bat Boat', the Supermarine 'Channel', 'Southampton' and 'Seamew', the 'Walrus', the Saro 'London' and in, later years, the 'Princess' and, of course, the 'Spitfire', to mention but a few of the aircraft that will be referred to later on.

There are also associated developments with a very strong marine aviation ancestry, such as the high-speed launches and the hovercraft, both of which more than merit an odd page or two. In a similar vein space will be devoted to the role played, in two World Wars, by the base at Calshot, which was originally controlled by the Navy, then the RAF.

Of course, none of this would have been possible without the dedication of a band of pioneers to whom the nation's gratitude should, eternally, be extended. It would be a monumental task to mention all of them, but the following are truly representative: Sam Saunders, Pemberton Billing, Scott-Paine, F/Lt Stainforth, F/Lt Kinkead, A. V. Roe, R. J. Mitchell and, last but not least, Lawrence of Arabia. I have chosen to provide pen pictures of a few of the old characters, all of whom I met

and knew except one, and my boyhood memories of that person are just as vivid as my adulthood ones of the others. A particular skill of the Saunders boatyard staff was the application of the materials needed to proof hulls. This was a method known as Consuta, a patented system of lamination whereby wooden hulls were made watertight.

New and familiar names are mentioned, at Cowes on the Isle of Wight where J. Samuel White and Sam Saunders became established, and on the mainland, with such names as Supermarine, May, Hardern & May, and Fairey Aviation; these and others are all included.

Finally there came in the year 2000 a proposed single-engined flying boat with folding wings that would be small enough to be at home in yacht marinas, yet purposeful enough to provide safe and speedy travel between resorts. Surely this project from a business at Lymington cannot be history repeating itself?

Being a committed romantic I hope that this book will recapture the spirit that enabled man, who had already conquered the sea, to master another element – the air. This mood can be summed up by the words of Constance Cumming, the actress, in the letter reproduced opposite: 'Indeed I do remember the flight to Madeira – it was the first time I had ever landed on water in a plane and I thought it was magical.' She continues, '...but most of all gliding down onto the clear water of the Harbour like a swan – what an entrance!'

The scene is now set, and I hope that the following pages will not only help to recapture the spirit but also the magic of the swan.

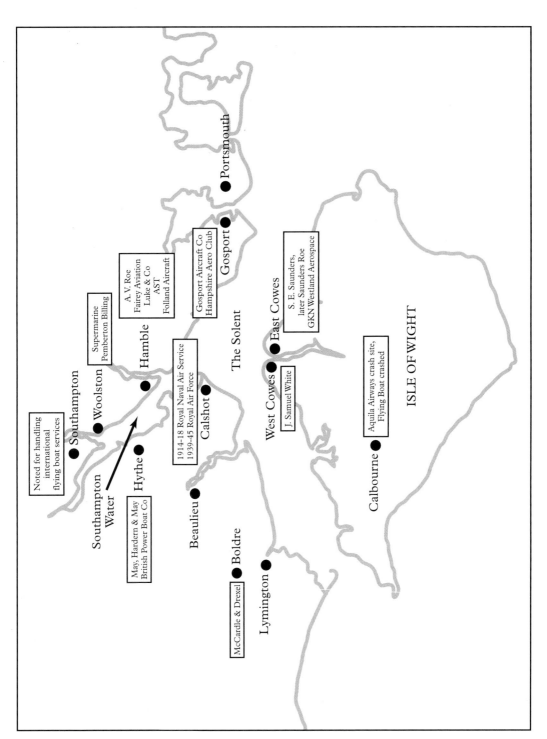

Sites of historical important to marine aviation around Southampton Water, the Solent and the Isle of Wight

1. BEGINNINGS, 1903-18

Afloat to fly

By 1900 man had conquered all the elements except for the air, but this situation changed on 17 December 1903 when the Wright brothers, in America, successfully flew a heavier-than-air machine and, a few years later, on 25 July 1909, the Frenchman Bleriot flew from France to England. These historic events must have inspired the likes of Howard Wright, J. Samuel White, Sam Saunders and the Sopwith company to design and develop flying boats.

My researches into marine aviation and, on a personal level, my family history ran on parallel courses as both took me to the Isle of Wight. I found that the early entrepreneurs were once located along the shores of the River Medina at Cowes, which, oddly enough, was the birthplace of my father. One such company, the boat-building business of J. Samuel White, set up an aircraft section under Howard Wright and produced a flying boat, which, after a number of setbacks, was shown at the London Air Show at Olympia in 1913.

The illustrations clearly depict the fragility of the early aircraft, some of which looked more like boats with added wings and an engine; certainly the outcome of the combined skills of S. E. Saunders and the Sopwith Aviation Company – known as the 'Bat Boat' – was appropriately named. This partnership owed much to the expertise Sam Saunders had acquired in perfecting the lamination of boat hulls. As marine aircraft then needed to be waterproofed this system of lamination became widely used in the new industry. The Saunders boatyard became busy producing watertight hulls for a number of flying boat projects, including the 'Wigram', the White and Thompson No 2 Flying Boat. A word or two must also be written about the pioneering pilots who had to sit in the open cockpit exposed to all sorts of weather. Apart from the physical discomfort they had none of the sophisticated flying instruments that are taken for granted in modern aircraft.

There were further interesting events in 1914, such as Sopwith opening a small factory at Woolston in Southampton. A short while before this Pemberton Billing had also opened a factory at Woolston, which was in effect the beginning of Supermarine. Due to production policy changes, Sopwith was to cease involvement with marine aircraft, while

The man behind Saunders Roe – Sam Saunders – seen with his wife circa 1913. *GKN Westland Aerospace*

Pemberton Billing also changed his occupation and stood for Parliament, selling his interest in Supermarine to Hubert Scott-Paine in 1916.

The Hamble River, which flowed into Southampton Water, was the home of Luke & Co, which in 1912 joined forces with another boat-builder and produced a floatplane that had a wingspan of around 100 feet. Sadly the business was financially overstretched with this project and later the premises were taken over for war work.

Thus, after a very short infancy, this new development of marine aviation found itself being called upon to participate in the national effort to wage war from 1914 to 1918.

Above **A 1911 photograph of an aero hydroplane invented by a Frenchman called Ravaud.** *GKN Westland Aerospace*

Below **The Sopwith 'Bat Boat' was built with a Saunders 'Consuta' laminated hull. In 1913 it won an award after completing a series of landings on sea and land.** *GKN Westland Aerospace*

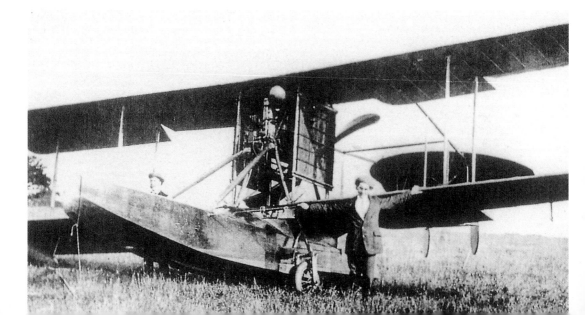

Above The Solent Works at East Cowes, a factory built for F. Bevis Ltd, which constructed aircraft there. Later Saunders Roe repaired 'Walrus' flying boats at the site. It was bombed in 1942. *GKN Westland Aerospace*

Below A view of the Cornubia Yard at Cowes where *Miss England* and *Bluebird* were built. Later, in 1942, it was used for work on the 'Walrus', and was another location bombed during an air raid. *GKN Westland Aerospace*

Your Country Needs You

When the 'war to end all wars' started in 1914 neither the Fleet Air Arm nor the Royal Air Force had been formed; one organisation was known then as the Royal Naval Air Service, while the Royal Flying Corps was the forerunner of the RAF. Thankfully these branches of the armed forces later re-organised and became the very efficient fighting units of the Second World War. While the military had a long history behind it, and was thus more able to change to the needs of the time, the new marine aviation industry had not been in existence that long when the Great War began. Thankfully it was mature enough to respond to the requirements of the nation – production methods were updated, companies expanded and the area saw new names, new factories built and the setting up of the Royal Naval Air Station at Calshot in 1913. This was primarily to receive locally built floatplanes and to test-fly them before acceptance by the service, and this local involvement saved both time and money.

It was not be until after four years of war production that the likes of Sam Saunders and Supermarine would be able to revert to peacetime development of aircraft for civilian markets. In the meantime at the Saunders factory there was considerable activity in the development of a two-seater floatplane for the Royal Navy. This work started shortly after the declaration of war, which meant that the aircraft was primarily a combat plane that could carry bombs as well as a torpedo. In addition to the manufacture of complete aircraft there were wartime contracts to provide specialist services such as the waterproofing of flying boat hulls. This was a typical example of where the Saunders yard made full use of its expertise in the 'Consuta' method that had been perfected originally in the boat business. In order to complete the work, Saunders found the need to build a new factory unit, which was opened about a year before the Armistice was declared. Although

Wartime production of the 'Felixstowe' flying boat at Saunders's Solent factory. *GKN Westland Aerospace*

J. Samuel White did undertake some aircraft work, the yard became fully occupied with the building of a destroyer for the Royal Navy, and this marine activity meant that the company did not continue accepting orders for further aircraft production.

The early floatplanes used by the Navy did not look robust enough to fly, yet the service pilots did just that and even carried bombs and torpedoes for good measure! In addition to the flight testing of new aircraft at Calshot, there was an on-going programme of pilot training. Time was also found for operational flights against the enemy, and before the war finished the annual flying hours of the pilots totalled several thousand. The base later changed from Navy to RAF control and it is not entirely surprising to learn that many of the functions performed by RAF Coastal Command during the Second World War were similar to those of the Naval Air Service back in 1914-18.

The war years saw changes and new companies making their mark. While J. Samuel White was fully committed to building warships for the Royal Navy, and Saunders and the Sopwith Company enjoyed lucrative aviation work on behalf of the Government, such was the high level of workmanship in the area that the Government saw fit to build new factory premises at Hythe, on the New Forest side of Southampton Water. It was here that May, Hardern & May, originally another boat-building firm, began the manufacture of the 'Felixstowe' flying boat. This aircraft was large for its time, its size comparing with many of today's aeroplanes, and its manufacture did much to establish Hythe as a centre for marine aircraft.

Thankfully the war came to an end, as we know, at the 11th hour of the 11th day of the 11th month in 1918. The world, and this quite special part of Southern England, could now start to return to the peaceful side of marine aviation.

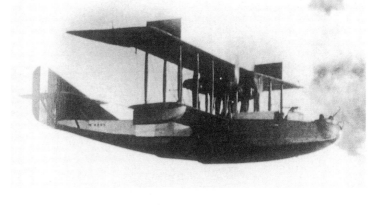

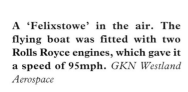

A 'Felixstowe' in the air. The flying boat was fitted with two Rolls Royce engines, which gave it a speed of 95mph. *GKN Westland Aerospace*

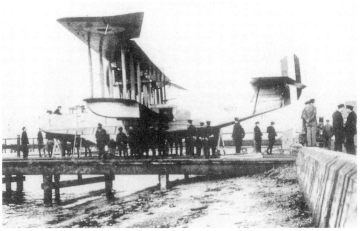

Similar to the 'Felixstowe' was the Curtis flying boat, for which Saunders built spare hulls during the First World War. *GKN Westland Aerospace*

A nice view of the Norman Thompson two-seat flying boat.
Twenty-four were built during the 1914-18 war. *GKN Westland Aerospace*

The 'Valentia' flying boat, developed by a partnership of Saunders and Villiers. It is still a biplane, but the hull shows the improvements made in later designs. *GKN Westland Aerospace*

Another flying boat that was born of a joint venture between Vickers and Saunders. This is the 'Viking' on the shore of the Thames; built circa 1920, it could carry four passengers. *GKN Westland Aerospace*

2. THE YEARS OF PEACE, 1919-38

Peaceful interlude

Undoubtedly the new aviation industry had gained financially by working for the Government, but there was an additional bonus in the advances made in design and production techniques. Now that the conflict was over there was a new challenge – to harness the potential to meet future commercial demands. Many of those responsible for the industry could not have predicted that another conflict would start barely 21 years later.

In 1928 a merger took place between Supermarine and the Vickers Company, and this was to prove quite important in future years. An early post-war design was the 'Southampton' flying boat. This was a biplane and first built with a wooden hull, although later models were improved with hulls built with a type of aluminium. The 'Walrus', a single-engined flying boat, was also developed and accepted for use by the Royal Navy; it proved a successful design and was launched by catapult from a variety of warships, as well as being used for target spotting and the rescue of survivors. The Supermarine Vickers Company also built the 'Stranraer' flying boat, the last biplane flying boat constructed by that firm. It entered service with the RAF and was eventually replaced by the 'Sunderland', designed and built by Short Brothers at Rochester in Kent.

Across the Solent, the Saunders Company carried on with its latest wooden-hulled flying boats, no doubt with the 'Consuta' method of lamination. These were the 'Valkyrie' and the 'Medina'; the latter could carry 10 passengers and fly at 115 miles per hour. There followed a number of unsuccessful designs and Saunders had to wait until 1934 before the A27 Saro 'London' began manufacture. After strenuous testing this biplane flying boat went into service with the RAF. The final deliveries of this aircraft, which was fitted with Bristol Pegasus engines, were made in 1939, and the RAF operated it on active service during the Second World War. As a point of interest, it was one of the types of aircraft flown by Captain Evans, who was later a pilot with Aquila Airways, about whom more shortly.

The Saunders factory was also busy with the development of an all-metal, twin-engined monoplane flying boat called the 'Lerwick'. This aircraft was also used by RAF Coastal Command, but did not gain the popularity of Short's four-engined 'Sunderland'. Other between-the-wars work undertaken by the Isle of Wight firm included feasibility studies into a replacement for the Short Brothers 'C' class flying boat; these evaluations continued throughout the 1939-45 period and did not end until 1947.

In the 1920s Sir Alan Cobham pioneered air routes over the African continent. These were used by Imperial Airways and were no doubt a major factor in the success of the services operated from Southampton. Sir Alan was also noted for staging air shows at local airfields around the country, and these did much to make flying popular with the public. This aviator and entrepreneur also perfected 'in-flight' refuelling, which was necessary for transatlantic flights made by the 'C' class boats.

In 1931 this country won outright the Schneider Trophy with a floatplane designed by R. J. Mitchell and built by Supermarine, with pilots and ground crew from the RAF. Not only was the prestigious trophy won, of which more in a moment, but the same aircraft also set a new air speed record. This brilliant designer went on to produce the 'Walrus' and the 'Spitfire', which was probably his greatest achievement. Sadly Mitchell did not live to see the success of the fighter; he did, however, savour the success of the Schneider Trophy.

The Supermarine 'Southampton', first built in 1925.
Two years later this type completed a 27,000-mile flight to Australia and Hong Kong. *MAP*

Of 1932 vintage, the Supermarine 'Scapa' was an
improved version of the 'Southampton' flying boat. *MAP*

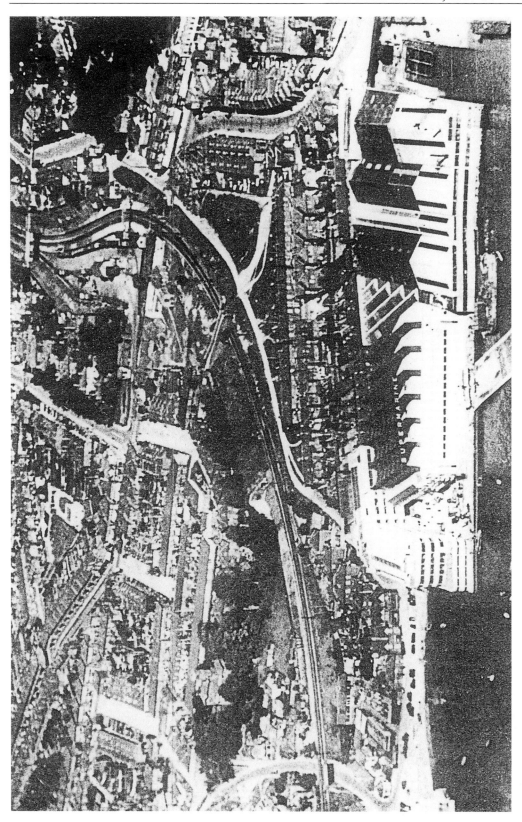

The Supermarine factory at Southampton before it was bombed. It was here that R. J. Mitchell designed several flying boats and floatplanes, although he is better remembered for the Spitfire, which was also first built here. *Southampton Aviation Museum*

Southampton was thus establishing a reputation for the handling of flying boats as it had already done so in respect of ocean-going liners. A massive jump in the size of marine aircraft from the early years was demonstrated in 1929 when the giant German flying boat made by the Dornier Company called at Southampton on a round-the-world flight. This aircraft was powered by no fewer than 12 engines and once took to the air with more than 170 people on board – remember this was over 70 years ago!

About ten years later two American flying boats called at Southampton on the completion of an eastbound pioneering flight from America; one was a Sikorsky S 42 and the other a Boeing 314 'Clipper' of Pan American Airways. The French national airline also sent one of its six-engined flying boats to Southampton to carry out in-flight refuelling tests, but when France was invaded in 1940 the aircraft was recalled.

In the 1930s there was considerable competition for mail contracts. Speed was of paramount importance, and the Germans used to catapult a floatplane from their liners in order to gain 24 hours in mail delivery. Likewise Imperial Airways devised the idea of launching a floatplane from a flying boat; known as the '*Maia* and *Mercury*' concept, the faster floatplane would detach from the flying boat and speed the delivery of mail by several hours.

By 1939 it seemed as if the flying boat was going to be the future of air travel, and most nations were constructing large passenger- and freight-carrying marine aircraft. The future of Southampton looked bright as the 'waterdrome' equivalent of today's Heathrow Airport. Sadly war was declared on 3 September 1939 and aviation developments during the next six years were going to change the world of flying completely.

Right Imperial Airways' 'Sea Eagle' G-EBGR, designed by R. J. Mitchell, on the water. *Adrian Meredith, British Airways*

Below right A rare and beautiful view of the Dornier DO X flying boat, which was powered by 12 engines. In 1929 it called at Southampton while on a round-the-world flag-waving trip. Once this aircraft took off with 170 people on board. *MAP*

Below This version of the 'Southampton' was built for the Danish Navy and was known as the 'Nanok'. *Southampton Aviation Museum*

Above   A fine late-1930s photograph of Pan American Airways' Boeing 314 'Clipper' *Yankee Clipper* moored off Hythe. *Stephen J. Dyer*

Below Another Pan American Airways Boeing 314 'Clipper' on Southampton Water after completing a flight from America just before the war in 1939. *Adrian Meredith, British Airways*

Photographed in about 1937 and high and dry at Hythe is a Sikorsky S 42. *Stephen J. Dyer*

The Saro 'London' and Captain Andrew Evans

This story is about a plane and a pilot, and starts with an aircraft that by present-day standards looked old-fashioned. The Saro 'London' was built by Saunders Roe; the first design was known as Mark 1, while the subsequent version, which was faster and was referred to as Mark 2, achieved speeds in excess of 150mph. Both versions were powered by Bristol Pegasus engines and a combined total of 31 were delivered to the RAF between 1934 and 1938. Unlike later aircraft this flying boat still had two wings, thus making it a biplane. Although primarily a reconnaissance aircraft it did carry bombs and remained in service during the Second World War.

The Isle of Wight company is remembered for producing several marine aircraft, including some outstanding examples such as the 'London' and 'Princess' flying boats, and had to combine marine technology with aerodynamic qualities to produce an aircraft at home on the water and in the air – a tall order. The special skills of the manufacturer also had to be matched with equally skilled pilots who were masters of their craft in both elements. One such pilot was Captain Evans, who first learned to fly in the Royal Air Force; his personal flight logbook shows that he flew the 'London' in addition to 'Liberators' and 'Catalinas'; he also flew on anti-submarine patrols and was mentioned in despatches during the war. After the conflict he joined Aquila Airways and, as a flight captain, was pilot in charge aboard the passenger-carrying 'Hythes', 'Sandringhams' and 'Solents'. He later left Aquila to fly for Britavia (British Aviation Services, a group of which Aquila was a member) and gained further experience on Hermes and Britannia aircraft before joining Ghana Airways to fly as captain on the VC 10s of that airline. His flying career took him to almost every part of the world with a staggering total flying hours in excess of 22,000.

Captain Evans was reputed by some associated with Aquila Airways to have been an excellent rough sea pilot as well as unflappable in the air – highlighting the qualities required to be the successful marine aviator he became. He had the honour to fly Britain's wartime Prime Minister, Winston Churchill, from Madeira to Southampton in January 1950. The former Prime Minister had been on a painting holiday on Madeira and needed to return to England because Clement Attlee had called a general election.

Above and right These extracts from Captain Evans's flight logbooks show his experience piloting the Saro 'London' (*above*), his time with BOAC then Aquila Airways, and finally the flight on 12 January 1950 when the Rt Hon Winston Churchill was a passenger from Madeira to Southampton (*bottom right*).

Left Andrew Evans in a Captain's uniform of Aquila Airways. *Mrs B. Evans*

Below A Saro 'London' in flight. Captain Evans flew 50 hours in such a flying boat. *GKN Westland Aerospace*

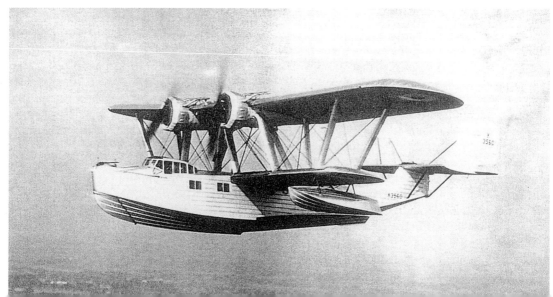

B.O.A.C. POOLE

								1520.25	**260.05**	**466.20**	**40.00**	**313.00**		TOTALS Brought Forward		

Date. 1946	AIRCRAFT Type	Markings	Captain	Engines. / Radio.	Holder's Operating Capacity	Journey or Nature of Flight. From	To	FLYING TIMES. Departure	Arrival	Day. In Charge	Second	Night. In Charge	Second	Instrument Flying	REMARKS.
APRIL															
15	Sunderland	DD 860	Capt Rose	4 Pegasus	Pupil Pilot	Poole	Hythe	10·30	12·05		1·35				Initial Dual
15	"	"	"	"	"	Hythe	Poole	14·00	15·45		1·45				"
16	"	JM 716	F/O Payne	"	First Off	Poole	"	14·10	16·12		2·02				B.A.B.S
17	"	DD 860	Capt Hallam	"	Pupil Pilot	Poole	Hythe	10·32	12·30		1·58				Circuits & Landings
17	"	JM 716	Capt Rose	"	First Off	Hythe	Poole	14·10	14·42		·32				"
23	"	"	Capt Harris	"	Pupil Pilot	Poole	"	10·34	12·06		1·31				"
23	"	"	"	"	"	"	"	14·00	14·56		·56				"
23	"	"	SELF	"	Master	"	"	15·12	15·30		·18				Initial Solo
23	"	"	F/O Bodger	"	First Off	"	"	15·36	15·54		·18				"
24	"	"	Capt Harris	"	Pupil Pilot	"	"	10·30	11·15		·45				Circuits & Landings
26	"	"	Capt Rose	"	"	"	"	14·15	15·00		·45				
								1520.43	**272.16**	**466.20**	**40.00**	**313.00**		TOTALS Carried Forward		

AQUILA AIRWAYS LIMITED

								1807·00	**1308·10**	**468·10**	**182·00**	**386·20**		TOTALS Brought Forward		

Date. 1949	AIRCRAFT Type	Markings	Captain	Engines. / Radio.	Holder's Operating Capacity	Journey or Nature of Flight. From	To	FLYING TIMES. Departure	Arrival	Day. In Charge	Second	Night. In Charge	Second	Instrument Flying	REMARKS.
14 FEB	Hythe	GAGIA	Pearson	4 Pegasus	P2	Hamble	Local	1345	1600		2·15				Circuits & Landings
10 MAR	"	"	"	"	"	"	"	1810	2215				4·05		Night Circuits & Landing

3771 · 40

								1807·00	**1310·25**	**468·10**	**186·05**	**386·20**		TOTALS Carried Forward		

								1808·40	**1312·05**	**468·10**	**186·05**	**386·40**		TOTALS Brought Forward		

Date. 1949	AIRCRAFT Type	Markings	Captain	Engines. / Radio.	Holder's Operating Capacity	Journey or Nature of Flight. From	To	FLYING TIMES. Departure	Arrival	Day. In Charge	Second	Night. In Charge	Second	Instrument Flying	REMARKS.
MAY 10	Hythe	GAGER	W/C Aikman	4 Pegasus	P2	Hamble	Local	1130	1220		·50				C×B I.L.
MAY 14	X "	GAGEU	Capt Pearson	"	"	Southampton	Lisbon	1130	1740		6·10			·30	I.L.
" 15	X "	"	"	"	"	Lisbon	Madeira	1100	1505		4·05				I.To.
" 17	X "	"	"	"	"	Madeira	Lisbon	1010	1430		4·20				1
" 19	X "	"	"	"	"	Lisbon	Madeira	1415	1815		4·00				I.To. I.L.
" 20	X "	"	"	"	"	Madeira	Las Palmas	1543	1758		2·15				I.L.
" 22	X "	"	"	"	"	Las Palmas	Madeira	1405	1655		2·50				Via Teneriffe I.L.
" 23	X "	"	"	"	"	Madeira	Southampton	0815	1800		9·45				
											34·15				

3809 15

								1808·40	**1346·20**	**468·10**	**186·05**	**387·10**		TOTALS Carried Forward		

														TOTALS Brought Forward		

Date. 1950	AIRCRAFT Type	Markings	Captain	Engines. / Radio.	Holder's Operating Capacity	Journey or Nature of Flight. From	To	FLYING TIMES. Departure	Arrival	Day. In Charge	Second	Night. In Charge	Second	Instrument Flying	REMARKS.
2 JAN	Hythe	GAGEU	SELF	4 Pegasus	P₁	Madeira	Lisbon	0922	1407	4·45				·10	23 Pax
3 "	"	"	"	"	"	Lisbon	Madeira	1002	1402	4·00					15 Pax
10 "	"	"	"	"	"	Madeira	Lisbon	0907	1337	4·30				·10	23 Pax
11 "	"	"	"	"	"	Lisbon	Madeira	1002	1407	4·05					7 Pax
12 "	"	"	"	"	"	Madeira	Southampton	0752	1702	9·00			·10		THE RT HON WINSTON CHURCHILL + 4
															Winston S. Churchill
16 "	"	"	"	"	"	Southampton	Madeira	2325	0800			8·35		3·30	SPECIAL CHARTER FOR
17 "	"	"	"	"	"	Madeira	Southampton	1115	2240	6·25		5·00		4·30	MR JOHN WOLSTENHOLME.
														TOTALS Carried Forward		

The Saro 'London' was developed and built by Saunders Roe in the early 1930s under work reference A 27, and complied fully with the specifications stipulated by the Air Ministry. These requirements called for low maintenance costs, the ability to fly on one engine, and a range of 1,000 miles. It took three years from the issue of the specification to the completion of a prototype in 1934. Modifications were subsequently made to the original design and an order was placed in 1935. The changes involved engines and air-screws, and the 'London' went on to replace older flying boats such as the 'Southampton', 'Perth' and 'Scapa', which had been in RAF service for some years.

The 'London' was powered by twin 1,000hp Bristol Pegasus engines, its wingspan was 80 feet, its length 56ft 9½in, its maximum weight 18,400lb, and its speed 155mph at 6,000ft. It was armed with three Lewis machine-guns and could carry up to 2,000lb of bombs and/or depth charges. The crew of five could live on board.

The 'London' was operated by UK-based RAF Squadrons 201, 204 and 240, while overseas it served with 202. In 1937-38 'London' flying boats of 204 Squadron were fitted with long-range fuel tanks, which enabled the completion of a 30,000-mile round trip to Australia and back.

A boys' hero

Sir Alan Cobham was very much a hero in the eyes of many of my age group. Unlike some aviation pioneers he seemed much nearer to the general public – at least, that is what I thought. Many years later I am very privileged to have this opportunity to write a few lines about the man and his successes!

I suppose the story starts as far back as the late 1920s and early 1930s when Sir Alan, flying a land aircraft then a flying boat, completed proving flights to the African continent. His detailed record of such flights was invaluable when Imperial Airways, then the national airline, started its regular service from Southampton using 'C' class flying boats; on these routes these fine aircraft were often referred to as 'Empire boats'. Incidentally, a brother of Sir John Alcock, the first pilot to fly the Atlantic, was a flight captain with Imperial.

Sir Alan Cobham is also remembered for bringing aviation to the man in the street. By demonstrating the safety and enjoyment that could be derived from flying, a lot was achieved in winning support for this new way of travel. He formed the National Aviation Day Displays, more affectionately recalled as 'Cobham's Flying Circus'. As a result of these air displays at provincial airfields, the public was able to see the flying machines and even talk to the pilots.

A problem with early long-distance flight in the 1930s was the inability to carry sufficient fuel, so a method had to be devised to transfer fuel from one aircraft to another, and after many tests Sir Alan solved this problem. He founded Flight Refuelling Limited at Ford in West Sussex, but because many of the initial experiments took place over Southampton Water it is appropriate to include it as part of our story.

At that time airlines were competing for the award of contracts to carry mail so it was imperative to solve the fuel problem. The flying boats were refuelled in the air from a modified Handley Page 'Harrow' aircraft used as a tanker; the 'Harrow' lowered a flexible hose to the 'C' class boat, which had also been modified for this operation. I remember watching such a feat over Southampton Docks. For Imperial Airways' service to America this method of topping up the fuel took place in the air over Foynes on the River Shannon before the flying boat set course to fly over the Atlantic.

In-flight refuelling was developed initially for civil aviation, but later, as airliners became more sophisticated, the need diminished. However, the company found that there was a military need and systems were developed that are still widely used by air forces of several nations. Television film of RAF fighters being refuelled during the Falklands campaign and the Gulf War is still fresh in our memories.

Sadly Sir Alan died on 21 October 1973, but thanks to his vision, civil and military aviation have been able to reap the benefits of his pioneering work of yesteryear.

A pre-war photograph of a 'C' class flying boat being refuelled over Southampton Docks. *Cobham Photographic Library*

Boats of the Empire

The 'C' class flying boat will always be linked with the local heritage because of an approximate ten-year association when it was used by Imperial Airways on services from Southampton. The manufacturer, Short Brothers of Rochester, Kent, had enjoyed a long period of success developing biplane flying boats for both service and civil use, included the 'Singapore', which was used by Sir Alan Cobham on one of his proving flights to Africa in 1928.

The 'Calcutta' followed, which in turn was followed by the four-engined 'Kent' with improved passenger accommodation that included toilet facilities. The 'Sarafand' with six engines was a huge flying boat for the day but that too was soon superseded by the new breed of monoplane flying boats known as the S23 'C' class. These aircraft were ordered by Imperial Airways straight off the drawing-board, such was the faith the airline had in the manufacturer.

A total of 42 of these new flying boats were built, many with a number of variations; for instance, some were fitted with long-range fuel tanks so as to be able to fly over the Atlantic. Two of these fine aircraft were specially modified for in-flight refuelling, G-AFCU *Cabot* and G-AFCV *Caribou*.

One variation was the modification made to *Maia* so that the flying boat could carry 'piggy back'-style a four-engined floatplane. The idea was for the floatplane, called *Mercury*, to detach itself from the carrying aircraft, and because it was much faster the mail would be delivered earlier than normal.

Unfortunately there were a number of mishaps with this class of flying boat. One involved *Corsair* when, because a navigation instrument failed, the pilot had to make a

---

'C' class flying boats operated by IAL

Flying boats transferred to other operators although originally UK-registered are not included.

G-ADHL	*Canopus*
G-ADHM	*Caledonia*
G-ADUT	*Centaurus*
G-ADUU	*Cavalier*
G-ADUV	*Cambria*
G-ADUW	*Castor*
G-ADUX	*Cassiopeia*
G-ADUY	*Capella*
G-ADUZ	*Cygnus*
G-ADVA	*Capricornus*
G-ADVB	*Corsair*
G-ADVC	*Courtier*
G-ADVD	*Challenger*
G-ADVE	*Centurion*
G-AEUE	*Cameronian*
G-AETW	*Calpurnia*
G-AETX	*Ceres*
G-AETZ	*Circe*
G-AEUC	*Corinna*
G-AEUF	*Corinthian*
G-AFCT	*Champion*
G-AFCW	*Connemara*
G-AFCX	*Clyde*
G-AFCZ	*Australia*
G-AFRA	*Cleopatra*
G-AFKZ	*Cathay*

Technical data

Type	S23 'C' class or 'Empire'	S26 'G' class
Engines	920 or 1010 Bristol Pegasus	1380 Bristol Hercules
Wingspan	114ft	134ft 4in
Length	88ft	101ft 4in
All-up weight	40,500lb or 52,500lb according to model	74,500lb

'G' class *Golden Hind* was refurbished after the war and the length was increased to 103ft 2in.

'C' class flying boat G-AFKZ *Cathay* at Southampton. *Adrian Meredith, British Airways*

forced landing in the Belgian Congo. The first attempt to fly it out caused even further damage and it was several months before repairs were completed and the flying boat was able to leave. After this incident the aircraft was refurbished and was once again operated by Imperial Airways, remaining in service until it was scrapped in 1947.

During the Second World War a number of the 'C' class were put into military service by both the RAF and the RAAF. Some were lost while on active duty, while others were operated on what were restricted civil routes during the war years.

The advent of the monoplane flying boat represented a new phase in the history of aviation. Their pilots regarded themselves in the same category as masters of large liners, as the onboard service provided by the catering staff placed these aircraft between an ocean liner and a first-class hotel. To add to this magic, each flying boat had its own stationery complete with the appropriate emblem. This reputation laid the foundation for a standard of service that was expected by passengers on later flying boat services and certainly added to the nostalgic mystique associated with marine aircraft today. One story from pre-1939 days concerned the 'skipper' of a flying boat who made an extra circuit before alighting on water in order that the steward could finish washing up in the galley. This was of course in the days before plastic trays, and

the steward was responsible for the documentation as well as the catering, which included silver service at meal times. These flying boats received considerable publicity, and, in addition to the normal media coverage, they appeared on cigarette cards and postcards.

Another pre-war class of flying boat, which was designed to replace the 'C' class, was known as the 'G' class, and the three that were built were named *Golden Fleece*, *Golden Horn* and *Golden Hind*. They were used initially by the RAF; G-AFCI *Golden Fleece* was lost in 1941 under RAF number X8274, but the other two, G-AFCI *Golden Hind* and G-AFCK *Golden Horn*, were released by the RAF in that year and operated on the wartime service from Poole to Lisbon. Sadly G-AFCK crashed on a test flight in 1943, but the other aircraft remained in service with BOAC until 1947.

Of the 42 'C' class built, most were operated by Imperial Airways, although some were re-registered by Australia and New Zealand and thus saw service with Qantas and Tasman Empire Airlines Limited (TEAL). No fewer than nine were registered with either the RAF or the RAAF and were used for military purposes. There were wartime losses as well as peacetime accidents, but 14 survived for about a decade before being scrapped at Hythe around 1947, while another two came to that end at Auckland, New Zealand.

Two 'C' class flying boats at the pre-1939 Southampton terminal. In the foreground is *Calypso*, with *Corio* bearing Australian registration **VH-ABD.** *Adrian Meredith, British Airways*

More flying boats at the Southampton terminal close to 108 Berth. This time it is *Cambria* with *Coriolanus*. *Adrian Meredith, British Airways*

Above Imperial Airways' G-ADUV *Cambria* is seen again out on the water. *Adrian Meredith, British Airways*

Below   RMA *Canopus* taking off from what is thought to be the River Medway at Rochester. *Adrian Meredith, British Airways*

A fine shot of RMA *Cambria* moving through the water at an unknown location. *Adrian Meredith, British Airways*

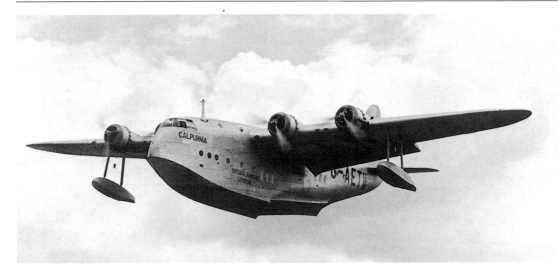

Top and above **Calpurnia** **is seen in the air, while a sister flying boat of the 'C' class is serviced on the ground at Hythe. The beaching gear is clearly visible.** *Adrian Meredith, British Airways/Stephen J. Dyer*

Left **Eamon de Valera, President of the Executive Council of Ireland, greets Imperial Airways Captain Wilcockson and the crew of** *Caledonia* **on 4 July 1937.** *Foynes Flying Boat Museum*

Above The modified 'C' class flying boat *Maia* with the 'piggy-back' floatplane *Mercury*, which was flown by Captain – later known as 'Pathfinder' – Bennett. *MAP*

Below Another view of *Maia* and *Mercury* at anchor off Hythe, with 'C' class flying boat G-AEUF *Corinthian* and an unidentified liner in the background. *Stephen J. Dyer*

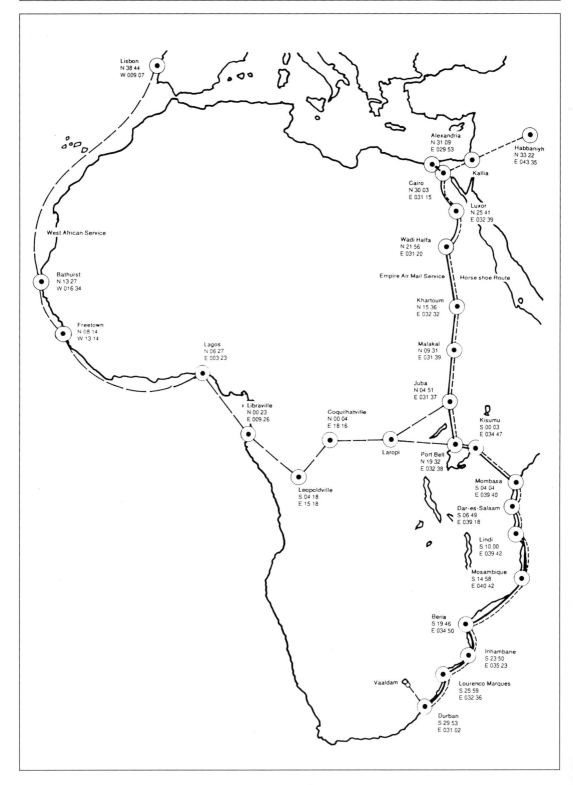

A map of the routes flown by the 'C' class flying boats. The mail service route was known as the 'Horseshoe Route' and the 'West African Service'.

The Schneider Trophy

The races for this prestigious international trophy started in 1913, and were the brainchild of Frenchman Jacques Schneider, after whom the competition was named. Early aviation owed a lot to this man, who was first inspired by the success of the Wright brothers in America, then, in 1910, by another Frenchman, Henri Fabre, who was the first man to take off from water.

Before this story unfolds it is interesting to recall the connections with local marine aviation heritage. Of all the races, four were held within the geographical area covered by this book; Bournemouth was in Hampshire when the competition was held there, and the other three races were held at Cowes and Calshot. A pioneer aviator, Henri Biard, was a test pilot with Supermarine and flight-tested many of R. J. Mitchell's early designs built at Southampton, so his participation in the competition was yet another example of local involvement in these famous air races; he won the 1922 Schneider Trophy Race in a Sea Lion

II, registration G-EBAH. For the record, the following were also Supermarine test pilots, although most were associated with the 'Spitfire' and later types of aircraft: Jeffrey Quill OBE AF FRAES, Joseph Mutt Summers, George Pickering, Alex Henshaw, Mike Lithgow, Dave Morgan and Sammy Worall Wroath.

There was another local connection in 1925, when one of the contestants was H. J. L. (Bert) Hinkler, whose house in Southampton was, many years later, demolished, shipped to Australia and rebuilt there as a permanent memorial to his flying achievements for that country. He is still remembered in Southampton in the name of a road through a large housing estate, Hinkler Road at Thornhill on the eastern side of the city.

A series of races such as these could not be staged without set rules, and a paramount one was that the course to be flown had to be

An aerial view of the RAF Station at Calshot, one-time base for Coastal Command and the Schneider Trophy team. *Southampton Aviation Museum*

entirely over water; as a result the aircraft had to be seaworthy as well as airworthy. However, the last rule proved to be an important one for Britain, stipulating that a nation that won three times in a five-year period would become the final and permanent holder of the trophy. In fact, Britain won in 1927 at Venice, and again in 1929 and 1931, the latter races held at Calshot in Hampshire.

From beginning to end there were 12 races in a relatively short space of time, 18 years, during which there were vast changes in floatplane design. From the quite fragile-looking aircraft of 1913 with a top speed of 45mph, they improved considerably with floatplanes like the Macchi of Italy and Britain's Supermarine S6B, which exceeded 400mph, setting a world air speed record.

Looking back it seems unfair that, though the race owed its origin to France, it was only won once by the founding nation, and that was the very first one, held in 1913. The international interest was always strong, especially so in 1914 when entries came from Germany, France, Switzerland, USA and Britain, which emerged as the winner. The

The Supermarine S4, which dated back to 1925. This aircraft crashed at Baltimore, USA, in the same year. *Southampton Aviation Museum*

course was subsequently changed so as to test the capability of the aircraft, and over a longer course the Italians proved to be fastest by winning in 1920 and again in 1921. The race in September 1919 was spoiled by fog and did not produce a winner. A British success in 1922 was followed by two American victories, first at Cowes in 1923 and at Baltimore, USA, in 1925. There was no race held in 1924, then in 1926 Italy was the winner with a Macchi flown by Major Mario de Bernardi at a speed of 246.5mph. Then followed the climaxing victories of Britain in 1927, 1929 and 1931 with Supermarine Types S5 and S6 floatplanes, designed by R. J. Mitchell, built at Woolston, Southampton, and flown by Royal Air Force pilots. In 1931 there was no opposition, so the trophy was won outright with a 'fly over' by Flight Lieutenant Boothman and the British team, who were serving members of the RAF. His speed was a little over 340mph in a Supermarine S6B floatplane.

All good things come to an end and with this ultimate victory in 1931 the South of England, and indeed the world, saw the end of a most interesting and exciting episode of marine aviation history that had affected Bournemouth, Calshot, Cowes, Southampton and the entire nation.

The SR 5 in front of the hangar at the Supermarine works at Woolston, Southampton, and on the shore at Calshot. *Both Southampton Aviation Museum*

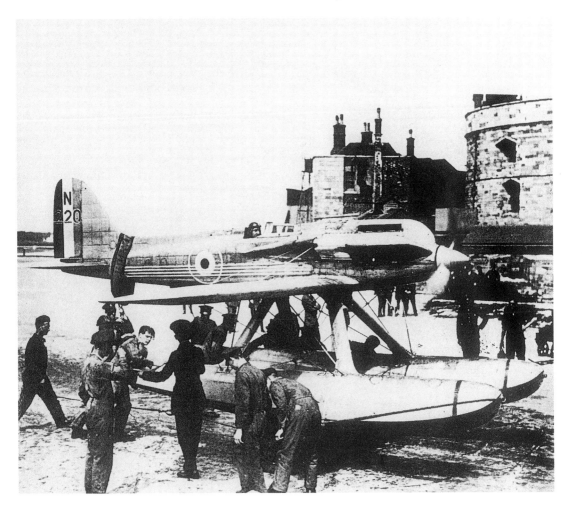

Above The first of the SR 6 series takes to the water at Woolston in 1929. The spire of Southampton's Mother Church can be seen on the far side of the river. *Southampton Aviation Museum*

Left and below SR 6, registration N 247, is seen from below as it executes a tight turn in the air and at rest on the water. *Southampton Aviation Museum/MAP*

Above The sleek lines of another SR 6, this time on dry land. Note the trailer and float supports. *Southampton Aviation Museum*

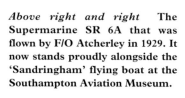

Above right and right   The Supermarine SR 6A that was flown by F/O Atcherley in 1929. It now stands proudly alongside the 'Sandringham' flying boat at the Southampton Aviation Museum.

Left A Supermarine advertisement that appeared after the world air speed record was set at 357.7mph in 1929.

Below The designer R. J. Mitchell, in plain clothes, with some of the pilots before the last race in 1931. From the left are F/Lts Long, Stainforth and Hope, while on the extreme right is Royal Navy pilot Lt Brinton. *Southampton Aviation Museum*

Right Supermarine's reputation for speed in the world of flying boats stood it in good stead for the 1930s.

THE
FASTEST TWIN ENGINED
BRITISH FLYING BOAT
(PEGASUS ENGINES)
"CLIMBS ON ONE ENGINE WITH
FULL LOAD."

SUPERMARINE

THE SUPERMARINE AVIATION WORKS (VICKERS) LIMITED, SOUTHAMPTON, ENGLAND.

Tiddley Winks

Flying boats in peace and war required the support of high-speed launches, while in war aircrew also relied on high-speed craft to rescue them when they had been shot down. These needs were fully met by Hubert Scott-Paine and his firm, the British Power Boat Company, based at Hythe, and the following account is but part of a bigger story.

In the early 1920s Scott-Paine was Managing Director of Supermarine in Southampton and was involved with the Southern Railway in operating an air service from Woolston, Southampton, to Guernsey in the Channel Islands. The aircraft used was a 'Sea Eagle', which could carry six passengers, and the pilot was a Frenchman, Captain Henri Biard, who was not only a test pilot with the Supermarine company; but also, as already mentioned, won the Schneider Trophy for Britain in 1922.

The Woolston-based company had built a number of flying boats, including the successful 'Southampton' designed by R. J. Mitchell. An important part of the production was the need for taxiing trials and test-flying of the aircraft, and the high-speed tender often used at these times was a launch owned by Scott-Paine called *Tiddley Winks*. About this time Scott-Paine also built a renowned high-speed motor boat called *Miss England*, and it was these two boats that provided the basis for

the development of high-speed launches with hard chine hulls. One distinction was the almost hygienic state of the engine compartments, which were painted white; any oil leaks were more easily spotted and this tended towards clean and more efficient engines. The British Power Boat Company progressed so much that by 1937 Scott-Paine found himself head of the world's leading boat-building firm.

Another internationally known figure – T. E. Lawrence – also became involved in the development of high-speed seaplane tenders, motivated by his having witnessed a fatal accident. When he was stationed at Calshot, 'Lawrence of Arabia', in the guise of 'Aircraftsman Shaw', tested seaplane tender *206* way back in 1931. The restoration of *206* in the 1990s was carried out by Powerboat Restorations headed by a dedicated person, Phil Clabburn.

The seaplane tenders were classified by the builder as the 200 series, while the larger 64-foot high-speed launches (HSLs) were classified as the 100 series and were developed for air-sea rescue operations. The fully restored *HSL 102* is yet another fine example of a Scott-Paine boat restored to its original condition. This particular launch was based at Calshot during the 1939-45 war and helped to evacuate troops from the beaches at Dunkirk in 1940. Thereafter throughout the war *HSL 102* put to sea in order to locate and rescue airmen that

© Colin van Geffen

200 class seaplane tender *206* was built for RAF service in 1931 by the British Power Boat Company to a design extensively tested by T. E. Lawrence as 'Aircraftsman Shaw'. *206* has since been restored. *Drawing by Colin van Geffen*

had been shot down, often making full use of a top speed in the region of 40 knots. In July 1941 the crew of *HSL 102* received a visit from King George VI and Queen Elizabeth, and 55 years later, in July 1996, Queen Elizabeth, then the Queen Mother, attended the relaunch of this vessel at Calshot.

The British Power Boat Company played an important part in our heritage story, but Scott-Paine suffered because of the untold pressures of work during the war years. Much of his time was spent in America and by 1946 he had to close the boatyard at Hythe. Sadder still, he died in 1954, by which time he had become an American citizen. In the 21st century it is still possible to see fine examples of the boats made by Scott-Paine at a purpose-built museum centre at Marchwood in Hampshire.

Left Another Air Sea Rescue Service launch, HSL *142*, is currently being refurbished and will again be a fine example of a craft once used by the RAF.
Drawing by Colin van Geffen

Below Sister vessel HSL *102* was built in 1936 and has recently been fully restored by the British Military Powerboat Trust.
Drawing by Colin van Geffen

Below Bearing a resemblance to the seaplane tender *206*, this high-speed launch was used at Southampton by Aquila Airways.

Below right This model of HSL *2754*, yet another type of Air Sea Rescue Service launch used by the RAF, enjoys a prominent position in the Southampton Aviation Museum.

3. AT WAR AGAIN, 1939-45

Wartime upheavals

The war that was supposedly to have ended all wars ended just 21 years before this country was yet again facing Germany. In September of 1939 no one could have forecast that the conflict would last six long years and in that time the entire world would be involved. Furthermore no one could have predicted the many changes that would take place. Before the war marine aviation seemed to have a bright future, but the wartime growth of land-based aircraft and associated facilities tolled a death knell for the flying boat as a means of international air travel, although for a time, at least until the late 1950s, there was still life in flying boats, with even one or two bright hopes thrown in for good measure.

The late 1930s witnessed an increase in flying boat activity at Southampton with a network of international services operated by Imperial Airways, and a look at the routes flown by this airline highlighted the importance of the port as a waterdrome. In addition to Britain's national airline there were proving flights being made by Pan American Airways, which in 1939 started a North Atlantic service using Boeing 314 'Clippers'. Another type of American flying boat to alight on Southampton Water at that time was a Sikorsky S 42. This flying boat was associated with Captain Charles Blair who later married the film actress Maureen O'Hara. Captain Blair founded Antilles Airboats in the West Indies and in the 1970s purchased two flying boats from Ansett Airways, the Australian airline; one of the pair is now on display as part of the collection at the Hall of Aviation, Southampton. There were further experiments with in-flight refuelling of aircraft and in 1939 an Air France six-engined Latecoere 631 flying boat was being evaluated in connection with this technique when it was ordered back to France in 1940 when that country was invaded by Germany.

The commercial structure of Imperial Airways was changed early in the war with the

Before the war started there were times when tranquil scenes such as these Supermarine 'Southamptons' at anchor could be captured, but it all came to a sudden end when the factory at which these flying boats had been built was destroyed by German bombs. *Southampton Aviation Museum*

setting up of British Overseas Airways Corporation to operate long-haul flights and British European Airways to operate domestic and European flights. The activities of both the new organisations were affected by the war – for instance, the Southampton base for BOAC moved to Poole Harbour from where a shuttle service was operated to Foynes in Southern Ireland, the starting point for a service to Baltimore in America. It was not until 1947 that BOAC returned to Southampton where the Dock Company provided a purpose-built marine air terminal at Berth 50.

During the 1939-45 war the need for more and more 'Spitfires' was so great that the Government directed the Supermarine company to concentrate its production solely on this aircraft and to hand 'Walrus' production over to the Saunders Roe factory at Cowes on the Isle of Wight. The Germans bombed the Southampton factory in September 1940 and the building was thereafter unusable. Luckily most of the machinery remained in working order and it was possible to remove it to a number of satellite factories that were requisitioned at the time. This dispersal of production lines was a triumph over adversity for the Supermarine staff who found themselves producing aircraft parts in one-time bus garages, a laundry and even car showrooms.

At the beginning these new venues were local to Southampton at Hursley, Newbury and Reading, enabling final assembly of the fighters at Southampton Airport. However, the growing demand for 'Spitfires' was such that a major production unit was also established at Castle Bromwich in the Midlands.

A considerable part of the Battle of Britain action took place over Southampton and the Isle of Wight, and in one aerial battle Flight Lieutenant James Nicholson, flying a 'Hurricane', was awarded the only Victoria Cross of that important stage of the war. Sadly this pilot was killed in a flying accident before the war ended.

Southampton received the full onslaught of the German Air Force, which made numerous day and night raids on the town (it did not attain city status until after the war). Apart from a few isolated attempts, the RAF base at Calshot only experienced the occasional air raid, yet from there it was possible to see and even hear the bombing in Southampton. The base had been on a war footing from the very start and had become established for the maintenance of three Coastal Command Squadrons – Nos 201, 209 and 240 – as well as a main centre for Air Sea Rescue and other marine craft, almost without exception built by the British Power Boat Company. The launches from Calshot rescued over 500 troops at Dunkirk and later in the war provided vital rescue cover for the D Day operations. In 1946 the 'Sunderlands' of 201 and 230 Squadrons returned to Hampshire and re-instated Calshot as an operational unit once more.

Saunders Roe and, to a lesser extent, J. Samuel White were again involved in the production of aircraft and components as part of the national war effort. The volume of business was such that Saunders Roe had to find additional premises on the island, in Southampton and even further afield at Beaumaris on Anglesey. A wartime neighbour of mine did a lot of contract electrical installation at Beaumaris, which meant that he spent long periods of time away from his home in Southampton.

The aircraft manufactured by Saunders Roe varied from the 'Walrus' to the 'Sea Otter', which was a derivation of the type transferred from Supermarine. The 'Lerwick' was a twin-engined flying boat developed by Saunders Roe, and although it was accepted into RAF service it was not as popular as the four-engined 'Sunderland'. Cowes, like Southampton, received attention from the Luftwaffe with one of the factories being badly damaged.

The aircraft that caught the imagination of the country was the 'Spitfire', which was subject to a multitude of modifications, included the fitting of floats and its evaluation for carrier operations with the Fleet Air Arm. A lot of work went into this, involving civilian technicians going to sea with the Royal Navy.

Back on the mainland the village of Hamble saw increased aircraft production, with a local firm, Folland, gaining fame after the war with the development of the Gnat jet fighter.

Neighbouring firms at Southampton Airport – Cunliffe Owen and Saunders Roe – were both engaged in producing a wide range of parts. Sadly during an air raid a number of workers were killed when a bomb hit the shelter in which they had taken refuge.

When the war came to an end and peace returned once again, with it came problems the like of which the world had not seen before. Southampton and the Isle of Wight were going to find the way ahead very different from the world left behind in 1939.

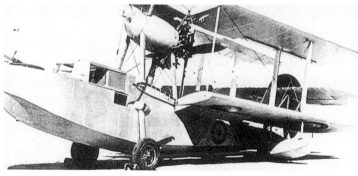

Above The 'Walrus' was an R. J. Mitchell Supermarine design and was originally built at Southampton, but due to the high wartime priority for the supply of 'Spitfires' the entire production was transferred to Saunders Roe at Cowes on the Isle of Wight. *Southampton Aviation Museum*

Left The 'Walrus' was a versatile aircraft that could be flown from land airfields, aircraft carriers and catapults. Its missions varied from target-spotting to saving survivors from torpedoed ships. *Southampton Aviation Museum*

Left A 'Walrus' on land. Note the wheels, which were retracted when the aircraft worked on or off water. *MAP*

The rugged design of the 'Walrus' is well displayed in this airborne view. *MAP*

When the Supermarine factory was bombed, 'Spitfire' production was dispersed to separate units in the Southampton area. Here are views of three such factories, each making a contribution to the final assembly. *Southern Daily Echo*

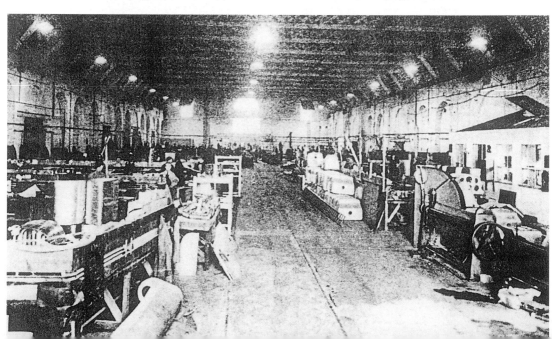

Sergeant Ben Brinkley

Ben Brinkley enlisted in the RAF as an apprentice at Halton, Buckinghamshire, which was a special station for training young entrants into the service, who were affectionately known as 'Halton Brats'. By the time they were posted to a particular unit they had received a thorough grounding in their chosen trade, in Ben's case that of aircraft fitter. In this capacity he was posted to Calshot just prior to 1939 as a member of 240 Squadron.

Sadly Ben died some little time ago, and it would have been nice to have had another yarn with him about his time in the RAF. This was not possible, so I am grateful that Mrs Doris Brinkley agreed that it would be appropriate to remember him in this way.

The story of Ben Brinkley very nearly ended during an air raid on Clydeside when his eyes were badly injured. Temporarily blinded, he was sent to St Dunstan's for eye operations and 'pensioned' out of the RAF. However, thanks to the skill of a surgeon his sight improved so much that he was received back into the service to complete his term of engagement.

The following are but two from a number of memories of wartime life at Calshot, where the one-time officers' mess became a public house called 'The Flying Boat'. One task that Ben was called upon to perform was helping with the beaching legs on the hull of a flying boat so that it could be beached or refloated; it was necessary to fix the legs when the aircraft had to be on dry land for any maintenance. To do this men had to wade into quite deep water, and at times a ducking could not be avoided, which must have been frightening for Ben who was a non-swimmer.

Another memory was of some rather mysterious fuel leaks in one of the flying boats, which were causing a degree of concern to the maintenance staff at Calshot. The leaks only happened when airborne and were never detected on pre-flight checks. In the end drastic action was called for, which meant Ben being strapped inside part of the wing when the flying boat was air-tested. As a result of this close in-flight inspection of the fuel system the problem was spotted. Someone had deliberately drilled

A wartime photograph of Sergeant Ben Brinkley, who was stationed at RAF Calshot during the war. *Mrs D. Brinkley*

holes in the fuel lines, then patched them over with wax, which melted after a time causing the fuel system to malfunction. Apparently the problem only affected one flying boat, and once detected there was no repeat and that was the end of the matter.

Before the war finished Ben was posted away from Calshot and spent time at another RAF station in Scotland. It was the skill and dedication of men like Ben Brinkley that helped to weave the nostalgic tapestry referred to as marine aviation heritage.

The 'Spitfire'

During the First World War R. J. Mitchell moved from Stoke-on-Trent to Southampton in order to join the drawing office staff of the new firm of Pemberton Billing. His talent was such that he was only 24 years old when he was promoted to Chief Designer. The company

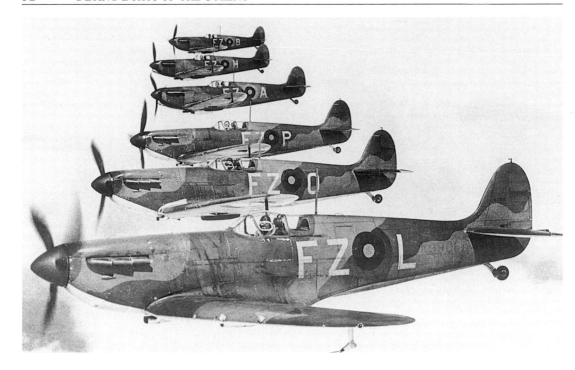

'Six of the best' flying in formation – early variants of R. J. Mitchell's 'Spitfire' fighter. *MAP*

later became known as Supermarine Limited, specialising in the development of flying boats and floatplanes. One successful design bore the local name – 'Southampton' – and some of these biplane flying boats were exported.

As the years passed Supermarine and Mitchell became heavily involved in a number of types of high-speed floatplanes for entry in the Schneider Trophy races, and by 1931, in accordance with the competition rules, the trophy was won outright by the Supermarine SR 6B floatplane. The same aircraft even pushed the world air speed record up to 407mph (see pages 37-43).

Further changes took place when, in the 1930s, the Vickers company acquired a shareholding in Supermarine and the new organisation became known as Vickers Supermarine. About this time development work began on a new monoplane fighter aircraft intended to replace the obsolete biplanes with which the RAF was then equipped. In the mid-1930s the company built another twin-engined biplane flying boat called the 'Stranraer', but in hindsight it was

provident for the nation that, in spite of harsh economic times, the company continued work on the new fighter aircraft. Many specification changes were made by the Government, but thankfully none were insurmountable.

There have over the years been doubts as to the exact date of the maiden flight of K 5054, the prototype 'Spitfire'. From a special report in the *Southampton Daily Echo* of 27 January 2000, it would appear conclusively that Vickers's Chief Test Pilot – Mutt Summers – took off from Eastleigh (Southampton) Airport in K 5054 on 5 March 1936. After that maiden flight there came a long programme of modifications, further test flights, the fitting of no fewer than eight machine guns, and so on. Just over two years later, in May 1938, Jeffrey Quill flight-tested the production model 'Spitfire', K 9787. With K 9788 these two aircraft were the first 'Spitfires' delivered to the RAF.

There were more than 20 variants of the original design: the engine was changed from the Merlin to the Griffin, both Rolls Royce-manufactured; the .303 calibre machine guns were replaced by more destructive cannon armament; and from an original speed of 362mph achieved by the Mk 1, changes in design raised this to 452mph, and this speed was

This is a later Mark of 'Spitfire' with cannon guns instead of the .303 Browning machine guns that were originally fitted. *MAP*

Preserved 'Spitfire' PK 683, a Mk 25, showing the two cannons fitted on the port side.

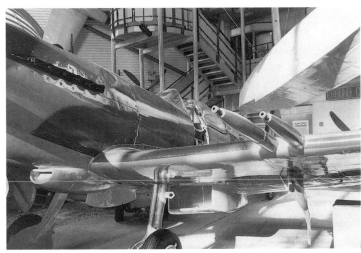

actually achieved by the 'Seafire', yet another variant developed for aircraft carrier operations.

From 1936 onwards a staggering total of 22,749 'Spitfires' and 'Seafires' were built, and out of this number between 190 and 200 are in private ownership today, of which about 48 are kept in an airworthy condition. Surely this is a fitting demonstration of the affection in which this aircraft is held worldwide.

The ultimate success of the 'Spitfire' owed much to the dedicated workforce of Supermarine, who overcame the bombing of the Woolston factory at Southampton and the subsequent dispersal of the production lines. It must have been a nightmare bringing tail sections, wings and fuselages together for the final assembly.

The 'Spitfire' saw service on a worldwide basis and was flown by the air forces of many nations, including Russia, and as previously mentioned there was a floatplane version, and it also operated from aircraft carriers. Thanks to the efforts of the civilian workforce and the pilots, the 'Spitfire' was a major factor in eventual victory in 1945, and no doubt in the mind of wartime Prime Minister Winston Churchill when he famously said in 1940: 'Never in the field of human conflict was so much owed by so many to so few'.

Sadly R. J. Mitchell did not live to see the success of his 'Spitfire', as he died from cancer on 11 June 1937, at the age of only 42. Although born and lovingly remembered in Stoke-on-Trent, Reginald Mitchell is fondly remembered also by Southampton, where the aviation museum is named after him and there is a plaque on a wall of the one-time Mitchell family home.

4. FLYING BOAT HEYDAY, 1946-58

· · · · · · · · · · · · · · · · · · ·

British Overseas Airways Corporation

This account of Britain's national airline includes the part it played in the Second World War as well as the period up to 1949 when it ceased using flying boats. The company came about shortly after the war started; the re-organisation of Imperial Airways was planned in any case, and it was unfortunate that hostilities delayed normal operations until after 1946. The forerunner of BOAC had connections with Southampton for a number of years, and it was therefore right that the national airline should resume flying boat operations from the port just as soon as conditions permitted.

Because of the war the flying boat operations were transferred to Poole Harbour in Dorset, and services were maintained from there to various parts of the world. For example, the North Atlantic route was via Foynes, the marine air terminal for Shannon Airport in Southern Ireland. Incoming transatlantic services terminated at Foynes, and a shuttle service would then fly passengers to Poole. This route benefitted from the acquisition of three American Boeing 314 'Clipper' flying boats, named *Bristol*, *Berwick* and *Bangor*. The crews of these aircraft received special allowances and were issued with non-austerity uniforms. This special treatment made their conditions comparable with their American counterparts who flew similar flying boats on the same route. Unarmed civilian aircraft flew to many destinations; RAF personnel were once airlifted to France in order to set up airfields for military use. The flights to the African continent often went via Lisbon where the difference between the blackout of Britain and the bright lights of a neutral country was most dramatic. A service was also operated to Sweden, a link that was very important because of the need to import ball-bearings. The aircraft used on this route were unarmed 'Mosquitos', which were very fast aircraft but not comfortable from a passenger point of view; if a passenger was carried he had to be strapped in the bomb-bay with a portable light, sandwiches and a flask of coffee or tea!

Some years before he flew with Aquila Airways, Prime Minister Winston Churchill made a flight in one of the Boeing 'Clipper' flying boats from North America to Bermuda, then to Britain; it was reported that the flight steward warmed the Prime Minister's slippers, this gesture no doubt making getting up that much easier!

The flight captains with BOAC were originally employed by Imperial Airways and many were devoted 'boat men'. Their names are now legend, and it would not be out of place to recall a few, such as Captains J. C. Kelly Rogers OBE, O. P. Jones OBE, A. C. Loraine, L. V. Messenger OBE, and S. T. B. Cripps DFC. Their wartime stories would surely make the most interesting reading.

It was not until 1948 that BOAC returned to Southampton and Hythe to continue from where Imperial Airways had finished back in 1939. By this time the Southern Railway, the owner of Southampton Docks, had completed the building of a specially designed marine air terminal at Berth 50 in Southampton Old Docks, now referred to as the Eastern Docks. This new building provided restaurant and bar facilities for passengers together with suitable office accommodation for staff, HM Customs and immigration officials. There were adequate arrangements for both freight and baggage handling in addition to the docking of the flying boats, which passengers joined or left by means of a gangway.

During the war, in 1942, BOAC had taken delivery of a number of converted RAF 'Sunderlands', and the civilian version was

A BOAC flying boat at Poole circa 1944. Wartime restrictions prohibited the use of Southampton, but sadly the national airline disbanded its marine operations not long after returning to Britain's premier passenger port. *Adrian Meredith, British Airways*

Short 'Solent' *Southampton* in BOAC livery at Berth 50 at its home port. After service with the national airline this flying boat was stored at Belfast until purchased by Aquila Airways as a replacement for *City of Funchal*. *Adrian Meredith, British Airways*

Southampton is being loaded with luggage at Berth 50 prior to departing on a scheduled BOAC flight. *Adrian Meredith, British Airways*

known as the 'Hythe'; the aircraft in this class all had names that began with 'H'. As these flying boats were phased out BOAC began to operate 'Plymouth' and 'Sandringham' class flying boats. By 1947 the pre-war 'C' and 'G' class aircraft had been 'reduced to produce', contemporary Ministry of Aviation jargon for 'scrapped'. The Corporation, as the airline was affectionately called, also operated some 'Solent' aircraft. However, by the time Short Brothers had produced the much improved

'Solent' Mk IV, the national airline had begun to favour land aircraft and was moving out of Southampton and Hythe.

The tradition of service, still very strongly connected with flying boats, was due to the dedication of the staff who had been employed by the airline for several years, and was continued by a new breed of pilot who, in many cases, had first taken to the air because of the demands of war. One such person was Captain Vic Hodgkinson DFC, whose story

Short S25 'Hythe' class flying boats operated by BOAC

The 'Hythe' was the wartime passenger variant of the 'Sunderland'

G-AGER	Hadfield	G-AGJM	Hythe	Many were sold to Aquila		
G-AGEU	Hampshire	G-AGJN	Hudson	Airways when the national		
G-AGEV	Hailsham	G-AGJO	Honduras	carrier ceased operating		
G-AGEW	Hanwell	G-AGKV	Huntingdon	marine aircraft		
G-AGHV	Hamble	G-AGKW	Hotspur			
G-AGHW	Hamilton	G-AGKX	Himalaya	Wingspan	112ft 9in
G-AGHX	Harlequin	G-AGKY	Hungerford	Length	85ft 4in
G-AGHZ	Hawkesbury	G-AGKZ	Harwich	All-up	
G-AGIA	Haslemere	G-AGLA	Hunter	weight	50,100-65,000lb
G-AGIJ	Henley	G-AHEO	Halstead	Engines	4 Bristol Pegasus
G-AGJK	Howard	G-AHEP	Hanbury		
G-AGJL	Hobart	G-AHER	Helmsdale		

Short S25 'Sandringham' class flying boats operated by BOAC

Also referred to as 'Plymouth' and 'Bermuda' class

G-AHZA	Penzance	G-AHZF	Poole	Wingspan	112ft 9in
G-AHYY	Portsmouth	G-AHZG	Pevensey	Length	86ft 3in
G-AHZB	Portland	G-AJMZ	Perth	All-up	
G-AGZC	Pembroke	G-AKCR	St Andrew	weight	56,000-60,000lb
G-AHZD	Portmarnock	G-AKCO	St George	Engines	4 Bristol Pegasus;
G-AHZE	Portsea	G-AKOP	St David		later models
					Pratt & Whitney

Short S45 'Solent' class flying boats operated by BOAC

Also referred to as 'Plymouth' and 'Bermuda' class

G-AHIL	Salisbury	G-AHIV	Salcombe	Wingspan	112ft 9in
G-AHIM	Scarborough	G-AHIW	Stornaway	Length	87ft 8in
G-AHIN	Southampton	G-AHIX	Sussex	All-up	
G-AHIO	Somerset	G-AHIY	Southsea	weight	78,600lb
G-AHIR	Sark	G-AKNO	City of London	Engines	4 Bristol
G-AHIS	Scapa	G-AKNP	City of Cardiff		Hercules
G-AHIT	Severn	G-AKNR	City of Belfast		
G-AHIU	Solway	G-AKNS	City of Liverpool		

First flying boat to Cape Town

In April 1948 a BOAC Short 'Solent' flying boat began a series of proving flights in preparation for a London-South Africa service that was to begin in May.

The flight of 30 April took 4½ days, and the total distance flown was 3,358 miles. The aircraft took 34 passengers at 200mph flying at 7,000 to 10,000 feet and was piloted by Captain Rotherham. It set off from Southampton – after a 7-hour delay owing to engine trouble – and carried well-known air journalists and some travel agents. One of these, Mr J. Hyde of Thomas Cook, preserved the documentation that now lies in the Thomas Cook archive and makes it possible to revive the details of this memorable flight.

The first leg of the journey was to Augusta, Sicily, a distance of 1,260 miles, accomplished in 6 hours. At Augusta the travellers stayed in overnight accommodation provided by BOAC and ate an Italian dinner consisting of Minestrone all'italiane or Spaghetti alla matriciane, followed by Dentice bolito (steamed bass) with Hollandaise sauce, then Tacchino (turkey). Next day's breakfast was served over Luxor and included bacon, mushrooms and potatoes.

To all the passengers the spacious flying boat with its comfortable seats, its bar and promenade deck, promised a future of luxurious air travel, which unfortunately was not to be fulfilled.

After leaving Luxor the aircraft flew to Port Bell, Uganda, with magnificent views of first desert, then jungle for everyone to enjoy. The flying boat then descended towards Victoria Falls, where the sound of water could be heard above the engine noise.

'We are quite close to the Falls,' wrote one of the passengers. 'The roar of the water is deafening.'

From Uganda, where the party spent the night, they flew on to Valdaan on the River Val near Johannesburg, their destination.

The flight cost £173, £23 more than a sea voyage.

From Thomas Cook Magazine

---

will be told shortly. There is no doubt that the magic of marine aviation also rubbed off on to other equally dedicated people like those in Aquila Airways, and thanks to them the flying boats continued in airline service at Southampton until 1958.

Captain Vic Hodgkinson DFC

There is much that could be written about a man who achieved around 25,000 hours in the air flying a multitude of aircraft types ranging from the single-engined 'Walrus' flying boat to the Boeing 707. In between there were four-engined 'Solent' class flying boats and the De Havilland 'Comet' airliner.

The story starts in Australia where Vic attended school in Sydney. After employment in the same area he joined the Royal Australian Air Force (RAAF) in 1937 as a storekeeper. In

Captain Hodgkinson looking very smart in his BOAC uniform. *Vic Hodgkinson*

Far left The cover of Vic Hodgkinson's book about the flying boat *Beachcomber*, which is on permanent display at Southampton Aviation Museum.

Left Evidence of the ongoing interest in marine aviation is demonstrated by this programme for the 1992 Flying Boat Reunion at the Southampton Aviation Museum. Note that the speaker's subject is the Saro 'Princess' flying boat, and visitors are recommended to visit the preserved *Beachcomber*.

1939 he began his flying career by joining a Flying Cadet course at Point Creek, Victoria. From there the tale unfolds with experience on 'C' class flying boats of Qantas and Imperial Airways before he arrived at RAF Calshot for a conversion course that included flying 'Scapa' and 'Singapore' flying boats.

In 1940 Vic joined No 10 Squadron RAAF at Pembroke Dock, and from there, and at times from Oban in Scotland, he flew on anti-U-boat, convoy protection and other operational missions. Then in 1942 it was back to Australia by ship, where he was soon in action against the Japanese and found himself flying 'Catalinas' on a variety of missions. Promotion and subsequent command postings came his way, but in 1946 he resigned from the RAAF as a Wing Commander in order to join BOAC in Britain. This part of his flying career was to last for 25 years until his retirement in 1971. In that time as a flight captain he flew flying boats from Southampton, and from London Heathrow a succession of land aircraft that included 'Argonauts', Bristol 'Britannias', Boeing 707s and last but not least the 'Comet'.

His flying career took him to every corner of the earth, and his qualifications are well worth a mention. In addition to the Airline Transport Pilot's Licence and a First Class Navigator's Licence he was awarded a Master Air Pilot's Certificate and became a member of the Royal Aeronautical Society.

In his retirement, Vic Hodgkinson has lovingly cared for the flying boat that is on show at the Hall of Aviation in Southampton; incidentally, this museum is due to move across the River Test to a new site at Marchwood. He has also swapped his joystick for a pen and has had a number of aviation articles published in magazines, in addition to the publication of a booklet about the preserved flying boat that just happens to be in the livery of an Australian airline. Lastly, while in the Air Force he was awarded the Distinguished Flying Cross and also mentioned in despatches for bravery in action.

For my part I am proud to be able to say that I know Vic Hodgkinson, with whom I hope to continue sharing many more laughs. My respect for him increases when he addresses me as 'My dear old mate'! The world of aviation needs more men like Captain Vic Hodgkinson DFC, who not only understand flying machines but are also excellent managers of personnel.

Five-star sky accommodation

In its heyday the flying boat offered just one grade of travel, and the fact that it happened to be first class was no accident. Silver service was normal at meal times, the food was served on china plates on tables covered with crisp linen cloths, and even the napkins may have had a

Flying back in time... Passenger comfort aboard an Imperial flying boat.. *Adrian Meredith, British Airways*

trace of starch in the laundering. The chinaware and glassware bore the crest of the airline, as did the cutlery. Pre-lunch or pre-dinner aperitifs could be enjoyed at the cocktail bar where a steward served drinks from optic measures. For the smokers there were even complimentary books of matches.

On some flying boats the onboard facilities were so arranged that sleeping accommodation was available so that passengers could retire during a long night flight; this added a degree of comfort that is today being offered as a new idea on long-range jets! The seating that was fitted 50 or more years ago gave the passenger more leg-room, and the Pullman-style seats meant that travellers faced each other and could partake in the art

of conversation. In addition there was always an abundant supply of warm blankets to add to passenger comfort.

Generally the service was of a standard that could be compared with that normally found on the large ocean liners of yesteryear, and this applied to the regular flights as much as to special ones that were referred to as 'proving flights'. On a normal flight from Southampton on the South African route in 1948 by RMA *Southampton*, BOAC served a selection of cold roast chicken, ham, cold tongue and roast lamb with various salad choices, followed by fruit tart and cream, cheese and biscuits, fresh fruit and coffee.

It was usual for the airline to invite guests to fly on proving flights, and in my time with Aquila Airways these were made to Capri, Genoa and Santa Margherita. As well as the onboard impressions

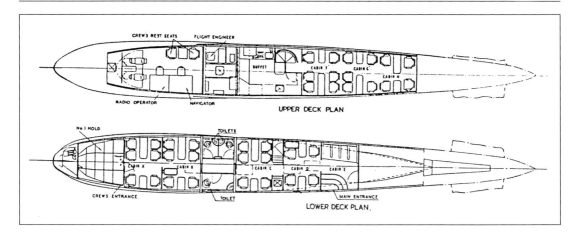

Above Aquila passengers were given boarding-cards during the check-in procedure. One side showed the seat number, while the reverse displayed a plan of the aircraft's two decks.

Below   Steward B. O'Neill serves coffee to a passenger on board an Aquila 'Solent' flying boat.

Steward George Barnes mixes a Martini cocktail in the bar of a 'Solent'. *George Barnes*

there were receptions arranged at the destination so that the press and travel representatives could judge the future appeal of the service that was to be operated. One such flight arranged by Aquila Airways on Friday 6 May 1955 saw the following lunch being served: Creme de Tomate was followed by Salmon Froid with Mayonnaise accompanied by a 1949 Chablis; then came Poussin Roti, Pommes Parisienne and Petit Pois with a 1947 Beaujolais, followed by Fraises Genoa, Fromage, Café and Brandy.

The normal breakfast served on Imperial Airways consisted of grapefruit and fruit juices, cereals, omelettes and bacon, and bread rolls and marmalade or honey. For lunch and dinner the meals began with a starter followed by roast chicken, pheasant or lamb cutlets with vegetables and salad, finishing with cheese or fruit salad. All meals were rounded off with tea, coffee and drinks from the bar. On Aquila Airways the meals were much the same with the soups, meats, bacon and scrambled egg being supplied in frozen form and heated in the onboard galley.

The flying boat was quite spacious and the ladies could use a powder room stocked with complimentary Elizabeth Arden toiletries. The gentlemen were not neglected as the cloakroom provided ample space for the hanging of outer garments. A selection of popular magazines was always available for passenger reading, and, when children were carried at school holiday time, the current comic publications were placed onboard.

A particular feature of flying boat travel was the freedom to walk about while in flight. Passengers were free to go the bar, visit a fellow traveller in another seat or to congregate in the promenade area. The two decks afforded quite generous exercise even if the aim was to lift a glass (or two) of a favourite beverage.

On long flights the schedule was so planned that travel was during the day, with a night stop at a first-class hotel, which meant seven or so days to reach Australia. This may seem slow compared with the 24 hours taken by modern jets, but it was quicker than the steamship and was a graceful way of flying that did not inflict 'jet lag' on the traveller.

One passenger whom I will always remember for his own brand of humour and true sincerity was the late Sir Harry Secombe,

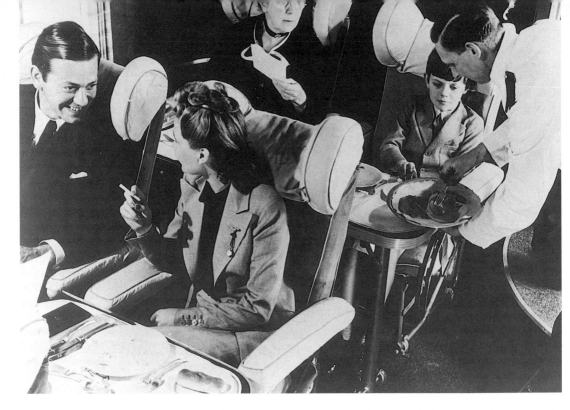

A BOAC steward serves a meal on board one of the national airline's flying boats. *Adrian Meredith, British Airways*

who travelled to Madeira with his wife and found time to talk and sign my autograph album. That was in the 1950s and nearly 40 years later he found time to write to me in support of my history of Aquila Airways, a gesture I shall never forget. 'Yes, I do indeed remember the flight which my wife and I made on a flying boat to Madeira,' he wrote. 'We enjoyed the flight very much. We took off with some apprehension at night time, but it was a nice calm evening and we soon settled down. Landing in Lisbon – on the river, of course – we ate a hearty breakfast on the ground. The arrival in Funchal Harbour was spectacular, and the whole trip was an experience we shall never forget.' Now that Sir Harry is dead I feel it proper that his memory should be included in this tribute to marine aviation.

```
                    LUNCHEON
                              Victoria Falls
R.M.A.Southampton             Vaalbank Dam.
Captain Rotherham
                  First May 1948

            Cold Roast Chicken
Boiled Ham          Cold Tongue
            Roast Lamb

                  -oOo-

                  Salads

                  Tomatoes      Eggs
Lettuce                 Potatoe
      Russian

                  -oOo-

        Fruit Tart and Cream

                  -oOo-

        Cheese and Biscuits

                  -oOo-

                  Fruit

                  -oOo-

                  Coffee
```

A menu from the early days of BOAC's South Africa route in 1948.

Aquila Airways

Aquila Airways was founded in 1948 by Wing Commander Barry T. Aikman DFC, an entrepreneur who believed that there was a future for the flying boat to operate to destinations inaccessible to land aircraft; 50 years ago there were such places, Madeira being a prime example. In the ten-year existence of Aquila the flying boat had an extended lease of life that had not seemed possible when BOAC disbanded its marine aviation operations.

Southampton was a natural choice for the UK base as the Dock Company had provided terminal facilities for the national airline. Aquila was able to rent a part of the building for passenger reception, and the floating dock was another facility that was on hand. After some searching, suitable premises were found at Hamble where the flying boats could be taken out of the water for overhaul. The head office was located in London, where the Managing Director engaged a small staff to deal with ticket sales.

The procurement of aircraft did not present undue problems at the outset because BOAC was disposing of its fleet of 'Hythe' aircraft, and for quite a modest sum of money Barry Aikman obtained flying boats and a quantity of useful spares and began the meticulous planning required to operate the service to Madeira. However, in the late summer of 1948 worsening East/West political relations brought about the need to airlift supplies into the American, British and French zones in Berlin. The flying boats of Aquila were chartered for this purpose and operated alongside those of RAF Coastal Command. Mainly two Aquila aircraft were used, a third completing a mere handful of flights to make a total of 265; revenue in excess of £55,000 was earned by the new airline. Sometimes three return flights were made by the flying boats. They loaded the freight at Finkenwerder on the River Elbe, flew along a narrow air corridor, often 'buzzed' by Russian MIG fighters, and alighted on Lake Havel, the Berlin terminal, in order to unload near the point where Gatow Airport was later developed. The charter arrangement was suspended when Lake Havel froze over, but with the flying boats being slower than the land aircraft they were not operated again when the lake thawed.

Part of Southampton Docks with a flying boat at the air terminal just left of centre and a ship in dry dock, right. This photograph was taken from a flying boat on a test flight – note the shadow on the water. *Vic Pitt*

Above **Another view from an Aquila flying boat during a test flight, this time looking down on the Hampshire countryside.** *Vic Pitt*

Below **Seen beyond the wing and float of a flying boat is the liner** *United States* **arriving at Southampton Docks.** *Dave Blake*

On 24 March 1949 the service was started from Southampton to Madeira. The maiden flight had on board a number of guest passengers, including the actresses Rosamund John and Constance Cumming (see page 8). In that same year a seasonal service to Jersey also began, but only operated for two summers. Later flights to and from the Island of Madeira saw Sir Winston Churchill and Margaret Thatcher as passengers on Aquila's aircraft.

In 1950 Aquila attempted to operate a UK internal service to Glasgow and Edinburgh, and the original fleet of 'Hythe' flying boats was enhanced by the purchase of a new 'Solent' Mk III – registered G-AKNU, it was named *Sydney*. This aircraft gave excellent service on scheduled services and charter flights up to 15 November 1957, when it crashed on the Isle of Wight with only 15 survivors out of a total of 58 crew and passengers.

Other flying boats were obtained, such as the ex-RAF 'Seaford', which was refurbished by Aquila and emerged as another 'Solent' Mk III in 1953, registered G-ANAJ and named *City of Funchal*. Sadly, in 1956 this flying boat was wrenched from its moorings during a storm at Santa Margherita and had to be written off. The replacement for this loss in June 1957 was a flying boat called *Southampton*, registered G-AHIN, another 'Solent' Mk III. In 1955 the

Aquila Airways fleet list

Short S25 'Sunderland' ('Hythe' class)

G-AGER	*Hadfield*	G-AGJM	*Hythe*	Wingspan	112ft 9in
G-AGEU	*Hampshire*	G-AGJN	*Hudson*	Length	85ft 4in
G-AGHZ	*Hawkesbury*	G-AGKY	*Hungerford*	All-up	
G-AGIA	*Haslemere*	G-AGLA	*Hunter*	weight	50,100-65,000lb
G-AGJJ	*Henley*	G-AHEO	*Halstead*	Engines	4 Bristol Pegasus
G-AGJK	*Howard*	G-AHER	*Helmsdale*		
G-AGJL	*Hobart*				

Short S25 'Sandringham' · Short S45 'Solent' Mark III · Short S45 'Solent' Mark IV

Short S25 'Sandringham'		Short S45 'Solent' Mark III		Short S45 'Solent' Mark IV	
G-AGKX	*Himalaya*	G-AHIN	*Southampton*	G-ANYI	*Awatere*
G-ANAK	Not named	G-AKNU	*Sydney*	G-AOBL	*Aotearoa*
		G-ANAJ	*City of Funchal*		
Wingspan	112ft 9in			Wingspan	112ft 9in
Length	86ft 3in	Wingspan	112ft 9in	Length	87ft 8in
All-up		Length	87ft 8in	All-up	
weight	56,000-60,000lb	All-up		weight	81,000lb
Engines	4 Bristol	weight	78,600lb	Engines	4 Bristol
	Pegasus*	Engines	4 Bristol		Hercules 733
			Hercules 637		

*Note: Most of this class was fitted with American Pratt & Whitney engines, but Aquila Airways' operational 'Sandringham' retained its Bristol Pegasus units. The reason is understood to be that this aircraft was originally used by BOAC for crew training.

'Hythe' class flying boats in storage at the Aquila engineering base at Hamble. *Vic Pitt*

AS.87/193/02

521

COPY

12th May, 1949

Sir,

I am directed by the Minister of Civil Aviation to refer to the application made by your Company to the Air Transport Advisory Council for an associate agreement with the British European Airways Corporation for a scheduled air service for passengers and freight between Southampton and Madeira via Lisbon.

2.   I am to inform you that the Minister, having considered the recommendations made to him by the Air Transport Advisory Council on your application, has given his provisional approval to associate arrangements between your Company and the Corporation for the above-mentioned air service on the following conditions:-

(i)   that the service will be operated with Hythe class flying boats at a frequency of one return flight weekly until the 31st October, 1949;

(ii)   that no passengers or freight will be picked up or set down at Lisbon for or from Southampton;

(iii)   that you will agree with representatives of this Ministry that precise operating conditions for the service and that, in particular :-

(a)   you will arrange with the Portuguese authorities for suitable and adequate air navigation equipment to be provided and manned at Madeira (Funchal) before the service starts;

(b)   you will prescribe limiting alighting conditions and undertake that the flights will not be made when there is an indication that the conditions at Madeira will, at the estimated time of arrival, be worse than those prescribed;

(c)   for this purpose, you will station at Funchal a person experienced in flying boat operations who could check the swell and indicate the degree of safety of the conditions.

3.   The Minister's final approval of the arrangements will be dependent on the agreement of the Portuguese Government and

/on the ...

The Managing Director,
Aquila Airways Ltd.,
6 Curzon Place,
Park Lane, London, W.1.

---

on the satisfactory settlement of operating and other detailed matters with the Ministry and the Corporation. I am to say that any expenditure or liability incurred by your Company in connection with the service before the final approval is given will be entirely at your Company's risk.

4.   A copy of this letter is being sent to the Corporation who will in the near future communicate with you regarding the terms of the associate agreement.

I am, Sir,
Your obedient Servant,

Signed J.W.L. IVIMY

Left and above A copy of a letter dated 12 May 1949 from the Civil Aviation Authority giving provisional approval for an 'associate agreement' between Aquila and BOAC regarding Aquila's new Madeira service, which had begun on 24 March.

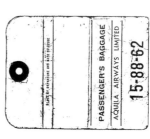

Left Both sides of a baggage tag on which the passenger's name, flight details and weight of luggage would have been noted before the tag was tied to the baggage item for the flight to Madeira.

	mls.	mls.	101	107	⊗	⊗	110	102	106		
							AQ				
dep. SOUTHPTON, Mar. ◆	0	0	✕ 00 15	✕			✕	✕ 13 00	✕	arr	
dep.⎰LISBON		917		14 00				13 10		dep	
arr.⎱MADEIRA, Funchal	1486	1525	08 15	16 30				11 30	12 00	dep	
arr.⎰LAS PALMAS	1822	1861	10 45					07 30	07 00 07 30	dep	
								15 30		arr	

SOUTHAMPTON — LISBON — MADEIRA — LAS PALMAS

AQUILA AIRWAYS—Short Solent Flying Boat
30 kg. (20 kg. Lisbon-Madeira and vice versa)—see note

provided at Southampton to meet specified trains leaving London (Waterloo) to convey passengers to the Marine Airport. Details on request

The timetable for the Southampton-Lisbon-Madeira-Las Palmas service from the *Air ABC* of 1956.

airline bought two aircraft from Tasman Empire Airlines; these were 'Solent' Mk IVs – *Awatere* and *Aotearoa* – whose respective registrations were G-ANYI and G-AOBL. The Queen had named the latter at Belfast in 1949 when she was Princess Elizabeth.

Throughout the life of the airline the flying boats were used on charter flights, with trooping charters being quite frequent. The longest charter ever made was in 1952 to the Falkland Islands, while the following year troop charters were made to Freetown and Lagos, and a ship's crew was flown from Helsinki to Hull. In 1956 flying boats completed a series of charter flights from Fanara (Suez Canal Zone) to either Malta or Southampton evacuating British people from Egypt. Other charters involved carrying equipment, technicians and even some of the stars in film productions such as *The Master of Ballantrae* and *Moby Dick*. Names that are recalled are John Huston, Richard Basehart, Leo Genn, Ossie Morris and Bernard Miles.

Aquila Airways became part of the Britavia (British Aviation Services) group in 1953, providing capital for expansion, as was evident from the purchase of the ex-TEAL flying boats in 1955. After a modest start to Madeira, a network of services emerged from Southampton to not only the island but also Las Palmas and Lisbon, and for almost a decade the flying boat was an umbilical link between Funchal and the Portuguese capital.

Flights were also made to Jersey, Marseilles, Capri, Majorca, Genoa, Santa Margherita and Corfu, which all helped to make Aquila an international airline. In 1957 services started from Southampton to Montreux, and regular flights were made from Marseilles to Palermo and Corfu in conjunction with Club Mediterranée. This expansion is borne out by the annual revenue accounts for the year ending September 1955 (see page 86), which, if an adjustment was made for inflation, would today place the airline in the 'multi-million-pound' class.

In total the airline had no fewer than 19 flying boats on its books, though not all at the same time. The peak was probably reached when the four 'Solents' were in use; these aircraft offered the air traveller a degree of comfort that compared favourably with the land aircraft then in operation. Aquila carried over 70,000 passengers and earned a rightful place in the marine aviation heritage of Southampton. The flying boats wrote their own part of this history when RMA *Hampshire* made the first flight to Madeira (see below), and RMA *Southampton* made the final Aquila flight to Lisbon on 5 December 1958. Barry Aikman had resigned from Aquila in 1956, and on 30 September 1958 all operations ended.

In 1950 Aquila acquired G-AKNU 'Solent' III flying boat *Sydney*. Here she is seen moored to a buoy and reflected in the waters at Southampton. *Vic Pitt*

Sydney photographed from another flying boat in sunnier climes,
and taxiing through choppy **Southampton Water.** *Don Townend/Vic Pitt*

Above One of *Sydney*'s engines is being changed at Berth 50, Southampton. *Dave Blake*

Below In 1956 *Sydney* made a rough sea landing at Funchal and damaged her tailplane. The crew members carrying out an inspection are (l to r) Engineer Don Townend, Captain Norman Leedham, Radio Officer Doug Hoyle and Steward Bob Woodward. *Don Townend*

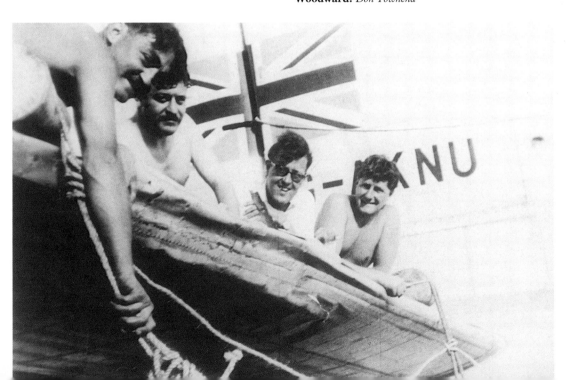

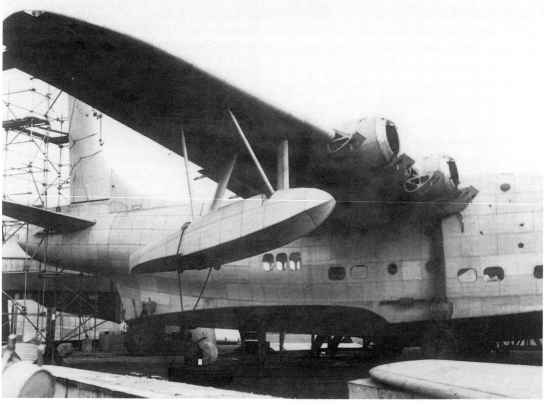

Left In 1953 an ex-RAF 'Seaford' was acquired and transformed by Aquila, emerging as another 'Solent' Mk III, registered G-ANAJ and named *City of Funchal*. This photograph was taken at Hamble during the major refurbishment process. *Dave Blake*

Below left Another view of the former 'Seaford' undergoing refurbishment. Every part of the aircraft was inspected and renovated. *Dave Blake*

Right Work is carried out on the tailplane of the future *City of Funchal*. *Dave Blake*

Below The conversion complete, G-ANAJ *City of Funchal* basks in the sunshine while moored in Funchal Harbour. *Vic Pitt*

This page In 1956 *City of Funchal* was wrenched from its moorings during a storm and blown ashore at Santa Margherita. It had to be written off. *Both Vic Pitt*

Above right Another flying boat that came to a sad end was 'Hythe' class G-AGKY *Hungerford*, which sank after an aborted take-off in May 1953. All the passengers and crew were rescued. *Vic Pitt*

Below right The wreckage of *Hungerford* was inspected where it lay near Calshot. Third from the left is 'Digger' Seymour, then Aquila's Chief Engineer. In the background an RAF flying boat can just be seen. *Vic Pitt*

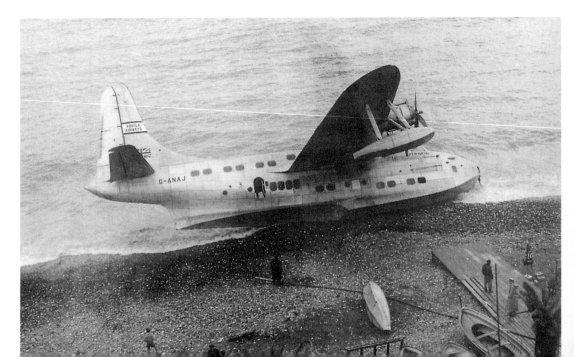

Left In 1955 Aquila bought two aircraft from Tasman Empire Airlines, 'Solent' Mk IVs G-ANYI *Awatere* and G-AOBL *Aotearoa*. On one occasion *Awatere* hit a rock in Pollensa, Majorca, and the salvage operation involved the removal of the engines to reduce the weight before the aircraft could be taken ashore for repairs. *Vic Pitt*

Below With the engines removed and flotation bags in place, the flying boat was towed to the quay where it was lifted ashore for repairs to be carried out below the waterline. *Vic Pitt*

Right *Awatere* is nearing the end of its repairs at Pollensa. Not long after this photograph was taken the flying boat was flown back to Southampton. *Vic Pitt*

Below right Sister 'Solent' IV *Aotearoa* is seen with the beaching gear in place being towed out of the water on to the slipway at Hamble. *Reg Oliver*

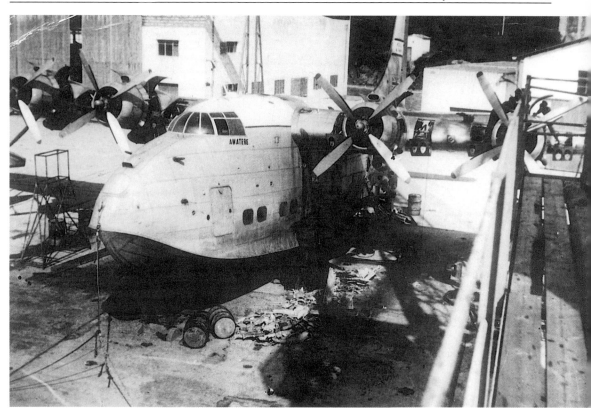

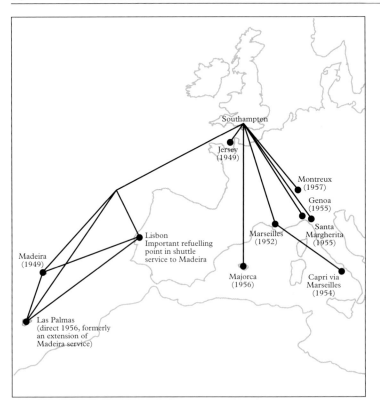

Left Map showing the scheduled routes of Aquila Airways and the year each commenced

Below The service to Capri began in 1954, and the celebrity passengers in the centre of this photograph are Capri residents Gracie Fields and her husband Boris Alpervici. The Aquila crew members are (l to r) First Officer Ken Hammer, Radio Operator Doug Hoyle, Air Hostess Muriel H. Lee, Second Officer Derek Weetman, Stewards B. O'Neill and R. Woodward, Air Hostess M. Evans and Captain F. Simpson. Other crew members on the flight but not in the picture were Captain D. Pearson, Radio Operator H. M. Bedford and Engineer Officer D. Blake.

PASSENGER MANIFEST

Owners or Operator   AQUILA AIRWAYS (BRITAVIA LIMITED)

Aircraft   G-AKNU, British   Flight No. AQ195/089   Date 20th January 1957

Point of Embarkation Southampton Marine Airport, U.K.

Point of Disembarkation Las Palmas, U.K.

No.	Surname-Initial-Title		Nationality	Ticket Number	BAGGAGE					Remarks
					Checked Pcs.	Wt.	Unckd Wt.	Total	Excs	
1	BEGG.	MR.	British	43758						
2	BEGG.	MRS. R.	"	43755						
3	JARVIE.	MR.	"	43761						
4	MACINTOSH. J.	MR.	"	27795						
5	MACINTOSH.	MRS.	"	27797						
6	COURTNEY. C.	SIR.	"	41256						
7	COURTNEY.	LADY.	"	41257						
8	CLUNES. A.	MR.	"							
9	CLUNES.	MRS.	"							
10	BRETT.	MR.	"							
11	McTURK. P.	MRS.	"							
12	STEWART-MASSON.	MISS.	"							
13	PHILLIPS. G.	MR.	"	41286						
14	PHILLIPS.	MRS.	"	41287						
15	BARNSDALE. J.D.	MR.	"	41093						
16	BARNSDALE.	MRS.	"	41094						
17	TANNER. L.	MRS.	"	41095						
18	SAXTON.	MR.	"	41095						
19	CLAPPEN.	MR.	"							
20	CLAPPEN.	MRS.	"							
21	BEW. S.	MR.	"	45582						
22	FARNHILL.	MR.	"	45584						
23	MINCH. V.M.	MISS.	"							
24	ANDERSON.	MR.	"							
25	FOWEY. E.	MRS.	"	45517						
26	VERRECCHIA. A.	MR.	"							
27	LADELL.	MRS.	"	1172/18149						
28	DOUGLAS-MENZIES. D.	MR.	"	45521						
29	DOUGLAS-MENZIES.	MRS.	"	45522						
30	COOPER.	MR.	"							
31	COOPER. E.M.	MRS.	"							
32	KIRK.	MRS.	"							
33	COLLINS.	MR.	"	45505						
34	COLLINS.	MRS.	"	45507						
35	HEFFERMAN.	MISS.	"	45506						
36	GUIRK.	MR.	"	45509						
37	COTTER. J.	MR.	"							
38	COTTER.	MRS.	"							
39	GRIERSON. B.	MR.	"							

CREW LIST.
Capt. Leedham
S/o. Squire
R/o. Whitfield
R/o. Iredell
Stwd. Hunter
A/H. Ackworth
Supy. Biddulph F.

AQUILA AIRWAYS LIMITED
PASSENGER LIST

All Weights in Kilos   Date 15th August   From 219   To Madeira   Aircraft Reg. G-AKNU

No.	Surname-Initial-Title		Ticket Number	Nationality	Weights in Kgs			Remarks
					No. Bags	Free	Excess	
1	ADDISON. H.	MR.	16997/8.	British	2	30		Las Palmas
2	CHINN. A.L.	MR.	16160	"				CHE
3	CHINN.	MRS.	16159	"	2	22		CHE
4	LEIGH. H.	MR.	17111	"				CHE
5	LEIGH.	MRS.	17112	"				CHE
6	HALL. E.	MRS.	17113	"	6	54		CHE
7	LYNN-ALLEN.	MAJOR	17040	"				CHE
8	LYNN-ALLEN.	MRS.	17043	"	3	40	2	CHE
9	IRAVRHCOH. E.	MRS.	16191	"	2	15		CHE
10	NESS. G.	MR.	17139	"				CHE
11	FRANCIS. N.H.	MRS.	17140	"	2	28		CHE
12	CHAMBERS. A.	MR.	15728	"				CHE
13	CHAMBERS.	MRS.	15777	"	4	40	14	CHE
14	GRIFFIN. N.	MR.	17088	"				CHE
15	GRIFFIN. A.	MISS.	17089	"	5	40	3	CHE
16	HIGSON-SMITH.	LADY.	17090	"	2	20	2	CHE
17	NICHOLSON. G.A.	MR.	16157	"				CHE
18	NICHOLSON.	MRS.	16158	"	3	36		CHE
19	REDINGTON. T.W.	MRS.	15770	"				CHE
20	REDINGTON.	MISS.	1577.	"	2	58		CHE
21	BEAR. A.	MR.	17153	"	1	14		CHE
22	BARKER. J.N.	MR.	17054	"				GRATIS
23	BARKER. A.	MRS.	17085	"	2	19		CHE
24	SCHERMULY.	MR.	17146	"				CHE
25	SCHERMULY.	MRS.	17147	"				CHE
26	SCHERMULY. G.	MR.	17148	"	4	80		CHE
27	SCHERMULY. G.	MISS.	17149	"				CHE
28	HARDY. H.	MR.	16196	"				CHE
29	HARDY.	MRS.	16197	"	2	36		CHE
30	HARDY. V.	MISS.	16198	"				CHE
31	PARNELL. R.S.M.	MR.	47488.	"	1	20		CHE 504
				TOTALS	42	532	21	

CREW LIST
CAPT. A.C.P. EVANS
S/O.J.M.LACKMAN
R/O.R.J.WHITFIELD.
R/O.J.MORGAN
STWD.N.MORAN
STWD.J.COULSELL
A/H. MISS C.MORGAN

Passenger lists for Aquila flights to Madeira on 15 August 1953, captained by Andrew Evans (left), and to Las Palmas on 20 January 1957 (right).

Above left Aquila Airways ground engineers Vic Pitt (left) and 'Nobby' Clark take a break from working on an aircraft at Berth 50 in Southampton Docks. *Vic Pitt*

Left Inside a flying boat at Berth 50 it's tea break time for four ground engineers. *Vic Pitt*

Above Refuelling an Aquila 'Solent' at Funchal, Madeira. Note the UK and Portuguese courtesy flags with the Aquila 'house pennant' under the former. *Don Townend*

Right When away from Southampton at an overseas port improvisation was called for when an engine had to be changed. Care was also needed – dropping spanners was expensive! *Dave Blake*

Below At Marseilles we see Aquila R/O Doug Hoyle (in uniform). The flying boat in the background is probably a Latecoere 631. *Vic Pitt*

Above The 'pilot's office' in a 'Solent' flying boat. *Vic Pitt*

Above right Former Aquila Flight Engineer Don Townend sits in the Second Pilot's seat of the 'Solent' flying boat preserved at Oakland, San Francisco, USA. *Don Townend*

Below During his days with Aquila, Don Townend (in white shirt) sits with local staff at Funchal. *Don Townend*

Right The cap badge worn by all Aquila Airways uniformed staff.

Right **Lola Soutter, a member of Aquila Airways Berth 50 office staff.** *Lola Soutter*

Below **Mrs Soutter later won third place in the 'BAS Girl' competition run by *Ferry News* in conjunction with Britavia, the British Aviation Services Group. In this company publicity photograph she is seen on the left standing beside the winner, Miss Sally Harris, of Silver City Airways' Passenger Service Division. Next to her is Eoin C. Mekie, Chairman of Britavia, Aquila's new owner, then Mlle Marcel Maeght, deputising for the second-place winner, Mlle Babette Corbin, a receptionist from Le Touquet Airport in France.** *Lola Soutter*

AQUILA AIRWAYS LIMITED

6, CURZON PLACE, PARK LANE, LONDON, W.I.

AND AT HAMBLE, SOUTHAMPTON

DIRECTORS:
BARRY T. AIKMAN, D.F.C.
LORD MALCOLM DOUGLAS-HAMILTON, O.B.E., D.F.C., M.P.
AIR COMMODORE A. V. HARVEY, C.B.E., M.P.
A. G. HOWLAND JACKSON, M.B.E.
B. M. KEMP-GEE.
BRIG.-GENERAL A. C. CRITCHLEY, C.M.G., C.B.E., D.S.O.

TELEPHONE: GROSVENOR 3947
TELEGRAMS: BOATING AUDLEY LONDON
CABLES: BOATING LONDON

RJC/JG.   17th March, 1952.

Mr. Peter Hunt,
Southern Daily Echo,
SOUTHAMPTON.

Dear Mr. Hunt,

    We have received permission to operate a service
between Southampton and Marseilles for the summer
months commencing on the 17th May, and finishing on
the 26th October.

    I am enclosing a leaflet giving details of the
schedule and fares. We shall be using either Hythe
or Solent aircraft depending on passenger demand.

    Please let me know if there is any further
information which you may require.

                    Yours sincerely,

Aquila Airways (Britavia Ltd.)

*Marine Airport, Berth 50,
The Docks, Southampton.*

TELEPHONE 23361

PRESENTED BY ....

This page A typical letter sent from Aquila's London head office to the press in order that a 'favourable' write-up would be published.

Inset The visiting card used by staff at Berth 50.

Right A letter from Aquila Airways founder and Managing Director Barry T. Aikman to John Hankin, writer of the Foreword to this book, concerning his 1948 Christmas bonus!

AQUILA AIRWAYS LIMITED

5 LLOYD'S AVENUE, LONDON, E.C.3

AND AT HAMBLE, SOUTHAMPTON

TELEPHONE: ROYAL 5989   TELEGRAMS: BOATING FEN LONDON

17th December, 1948.

J. Hankin, Esq.,
39, Howard Road,
SOUTHAMPTON.

Dear *Hankin*

    This is just a line to wish you a Merry Christmas and
to tell you that the Board have authorised a Christmas bonus
for 1948 amounting to one week's salary for every three
months' service with the Company up to 25th December 1948 or
pro rata.

    If you wish to receive the bonus in cash it will I am
afraid rank as taxable income. If, however, you would like
to obtain the benefit of the Christmas bonus free of income
tax this could be arranged by your submitting to the Secretary
vouchers in respect of purchases totalling not less than the
amount of your bonus.

    The gross amount of your Christmas bonus is £13. 1. 9d.
Will you please advise the Secretary, Mr. P. A. Aldrich, as
soon as possible, whether you wish to draw your Christmas
bonus in cash or in kind as outlined above.

Yours *sincerely*

[signature]

BTA/KH:

Appendix

Charter Rates agreed per Board Meeting 15 June 1948

Ordinary Rate   8/- per nautical mile
Time Charter

1.	Daily	£150	) + 4/- per nautical mile - such
2.	Monthly	£3000	) mileage not to exceed 20000 in
3.	Quarterly	£8000	) any consecutive days.
4.	Half Year	£15000	)

Passenger

Ordinary Rate   10/6 per nautical mile
Time Charter

1.	Daily	£162	) + 4/6 per nautical mile - such
2.	Monthly	£3375	) mileage not to exceed 20000 in
3.	Quarterly	£9000	) any 30 consecutive days plus
4.	Half Year	£17000	) handling charges.

- - - - - - - - - - -

Aircraft Income   11 Months to 30 June 1949

Scheduled Service

Madeira	£ 2917
Passenger Charter	3814
Freight Charter	1749
Berlin Airlift	54423
Positioning	2975
Demmurrage	6535
Total	£72413

Aircraft: G-AHEO G-AGIA G-AGER G-AGEU G-AGKX G-AGKY

- - - - - - - - - - -

Operating Account for Year End 30 September 1955
Revenue

	£
Passengers	291277
Excess Baggage	3276
Mail	7046
Freight	3646
Subsidy	13095
Commission	853
Charter	13775
Bar Takings	3215
Cancelled Fees	527
Incidentals	29
	336751

Direct Costs
Included were:

Aircraft Hire	6531	
Fuel	81706	
Handling	21506	
Aircrew	7099	
Catering	10120	
Overhauls	48041	
Commission Paid	22784	206970
Gross Operating Profit		129781
Indirect Operating Costs		84885
Net Operating Profit		44895
Overhead Expenses		50129
Net Loss		5233
Included in Overheads		
Salaries - £11929		
Genoa Proving Flight		1323
Balance to Profit and		
Loss A/C		6556

Details of charter rates and financial information for the year ending 30 September 1955 as referred to in the text.

The Season's Greetings from Aquila.

Treyer Evans, father of Captain Andrew Evans, was a man of many talents, and one year painted this delightful picture for an Aquila Airways Christmas card.

Above 'Solent' Mk III *Southampton* was the replacement for the ill-fated *City of Funchal*, and is seen here having just left the pontoon at Berth 50. It will soon be under power in order to proceed to the take-off area further down Southampton Water.

Below Flight checks completed, Captain Norman Leedham has started the outer engines ready for take-off on this delivery flight to Lisbon on 20 December 1958. This was the last departure of an Aquila Airways flying boat and in effect brought the company to an end after a life of ten years.

Captain Jim Broadbent

In the 1950s Captain Broadbent flew land aircraft for another airline that was in that same group of companies as Aquila, and in order to maintain the marine endorsement on his pilot's licence he used to arrange a short secondment in order to fly the required number of hours needed for the extra qualification. After a period of time he eventually joined Aquila on a permanent contract.

However, this story goes back to 25 March 1910 when he was born at Eastbourne in England, and christened Harry Frank Broadbent. After the death of his father, his mother remarried and the family moved to Australia. He originally seemed destined to be a farmer and attended an agricultural college, but managed to learn to fly in 1929. Flying then became a major part of his life, and in the 1930s he took part in a number of air races and was not deterred by being censured by the Australian Aviation Authorities in 1933 for flying alongside the American liner *Mariposa* as it sailed under the then new Sydney Harbour Bridge.

In 1935 the pioneering aviator Sir Charles Kingsford Smith was lost on a flight to Australia, and in the same year Jim took delivery of a Percival Gull aircraft and flew it from the UK to Australia in the solo record time of 6 days, 21 hours and 19 minutes. This record did not last long as a short while later, on 5 October 1936, Jean Batten left Britain to fly to New Zealand, reaching Darwin in 5 days, 21 hours and 3 minutes, beating Jim Broadbent by a whole day.

At one point in his life Jim forsook aviation in order to own and train racehorses, and it must be said that he enjoyed some success in this completely different vocation. However, this career did not last and he returned to flying. In 1937 he flew to England in 6 days and 8 hours; later, in a different aircraft, he made the same journey in a new solo record time of 5 days and 4 hours.

Just before the outbreak of war in 1939 he was a first officer with Qantas on the Empire Flying Boat service between Singapore and Sydney; this sector extended the Empire link forged by Imperial Airways from England to Singapore with the 'C' class flying boat. The war years saw Jim ferrying a variety of aircraft from Canada to England and also from America to Australia. In 1944 he was pilot in charge of an aircraft carrying American servicemen, and when both engines failed he had to make an emergency landing, successfully accomplished on a sandy beach.

Taken at Lisbon in 1958, a quintet of Aquila aircrew: (l to r) Engineer Bill Cole, Captain Jim Broadbent, Second Officer John Squires (in a Silver City uniform), First Officer Pat Holt and Senior Flight Engineer Eric Iredell. *Don Townend*

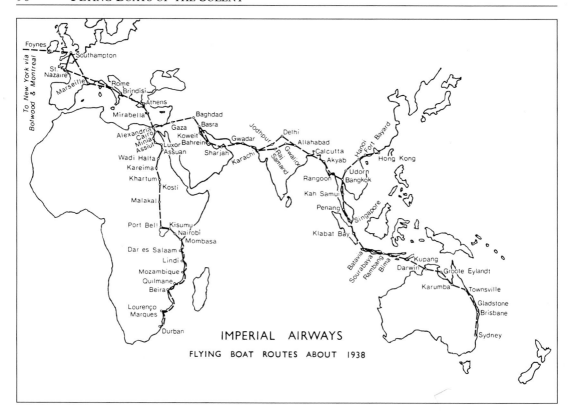

IMPERIAL AIRWAYS

FLYING BOAT ROUTES ABOUT 1938

In 1939 Jim was a First Officer with Qantas on the Empire Flying Boat service between Singapore and Sydney; Qantas usually operated the final sector of Imperial Airways' route to Australia.

During his career with Aquila Airways, Captain Broadbent flew, as pilot in charge, on all of the routes that were operated, and when the airline closed down in 1958 he flew Martin Mariner flying boats for the Portuguese airline that had been formed to operate a service from Lisbon to Madeira.

The fortune that had for so long been on the side of a pilot who had totalled over 10,600 hours in command of marine aircraft deserted him on 9 November 1958 when his Martin Mariner crashed shortly after take-off from Lisbon; there were no survivors or debris. Jim Broadbent was probably the last of a long line of pioneer aviators to be lost at sea, never to be found. In coming to this tragic end he joined an illustrious list that included the likes of Charles Ulm, George Littlejohn, Kingsford Smith, Amelia Earhart and Amy Johnson.

The Southampton Water fireboat

This important safety measure was provided at Southampton from the end of November 1950 until 1 January 1956, during which time fire cover was provided for a total of 937 aircraft movements, while the reports for the period 1956-59 reveal that cover was provided for only a total of 29 aircraft movements. The safety cover was then provided by the Southampton Fire Brigade, which today is part of the Hampshire Fire & Rescue Service.

This very important part of aviation is all too often overlooked and is only mentioned when there is an accident. The relevant Brigade Order Number 81/1950 (reproduced here) sets out the full details of the procedures to be followed by the crew of the fireboat; for instance, under 'Communications with the Fireboat whilst on Aircraft Cover' it is made clear with whom the fireboat should be in R/T contact. It goes on to stipulate the manning level, which was set at a minimum of five, including one officer, and when the crew

BRIGADE ORDER NO. 81/1950.

FIRE BOAT COVER TO 'AQUILA AIRWAYS' FLYING BOATS

1. As from Monday, 27th November, 1950, the Southampton Fire Brigade becomes responsible for providing fire and rescue cover for all arrivals, departures and test flights by Aquila Airways Flying Boats. The cover will be provided by Fireboat No. 27 and when engaged upon this service the Fireboat will not be available for any other incident except in the special circumstances detailed in paragraph 8.

2. **Control Procedure.**

   Receipt of Information of an Aircraft Movement.

   The notification of an aircraft movement will come from the Harbour Masters Office to the Officer in charge, New Dock Station, and will comprise the following information, namely:-

   Estimated time of touch down or take off.
   Estimated area of operation.
   Any other information, e.g., weather conditions, etc.

   It will be the responsibility of the Officer in charge, New Dock, to inform Headquarters Control of the estimated time of the operation and area, also any amendments to the initial message.

   Form F.D.31, 'Aircraft Movement Message' containing all the above information will be completed at the New Dock and Central Control. Headquarters Control will be responsible for informing Woolston Control when the Fireboat is not available due to aircraft cover.

3. **Communications with the Fireboat while on Aircraft Cover.**

   The Fireboat will be equipped with additional R.T. equipment on the aircraft frequency, but due to the limitations of the battery capacity of the Boat and the possibility of interference it may be impossible to use both Fire Service and aircraft frequencies together. The Boat will remain on the Fire Service frequency until she arrives at her station on the flarepath, when she will report off the Fire Service frequency in the normal manner and report on the aircraft frequency, on which she will remain until returning to her berth, with the exception of an half-hourly report on the Fire Service frequency to Headquarters Control (H2HW..) for transmission or reception of non-urgent messages.

   Should it become necessary to send an urgent emergency message to the Fireboat while on aircraft cover, the message may be sent by telephone to the Control Officer, Southampton Airport Control, Eastleigh, Tele: No: 87226, who will transmit on the aircraft frequency to the Fireboat via the Control Launch. The above procedure for emergency messages may only be used with the sanction of the Chief or Deputy Chief Officer.

4. **Operational Procedure.**

   Manning.

   The strength of the Fireboat crew for aircraft cover must not be less than five men and must include one Officer, e.g., Leading Fireman or above.

5. **Action on Proceeding to Aircraft Cover.**

   An additional No. 2. Foam branch and knapsack tank is to be put aboard, this will be on loan from Tender No. 25 and is to be returned at the end of the operation.

   The skiff will not be towed, it is to be secured to the pontoon and in the safest manner possible, having regard to tide, wind and sea conditions during the period the Fireboat will be away from berth. Additional first aid equipment will be picked up from the Gate House, Royal Pier.

   /6.

6. **Position of Fireboat in Relation to Flarepath and Aircraft.**

   The Fireboat's position is on the port hand side of, and about midway along, the flarepath. The Officer in charge is to position the Fireboat so that she is opposite to and heading toward the estimated position of the aircraft at the end of the 'touch down' or when 'taking off', the point at which she becomes airborne.

   After the departure of an aircraft the regulations require that the emergency craft should stay on their stations until the aircraft has reached 'her point of no return'. The Officer in charge Fireboat, should be guided on this point by the Control Officer aboard the Control Launch.

   Should the aircraft be forced to return after the Fireboat has returned to her station, Southampton Airport Control will inform Headquarters Control and the Fireboat will be ordered back to the landing area.

7. **Wearing of Lifejackets by Crew on Aircraft Cover.**

   The wearing of lifejackets is left to the discretion of the Officer in charge of the Fireboat, who should bear in mind the very limited deck space of the Fireboat, also that the boat may be operating in relatively exposed waters.

   The Officer in charge, Fireboat, would be well advised to order 'lifejackets on' prior to tackling a fire on a flying boat.

8. **Action to be Taken when Fireboat is not available or has to be withdrawn.**

   The Fireboat will only be withdrawn from aircraft cover on the specific instructions of the Chief Officer or Deputy Chief Officer. When it is known that the Fireboat will not be available, or has to be withdrawn, the following action must be taken:-

   a) Contact is to be made with Messrs. Matthews Bros., Tele: No: 3483, and a launch ordered to the Fireboat berth. At the sametime, the following equipment will be ordered from the Dock and Central Stations to the Berth, namely:-

      Light Pump No. 37.   (Docks).
      4 - lengths rubber lined hose.   (Docks).
      1 - No. 2. Foam Branch & Knapsack Tank.   (Central).
      20 - galls. Foam Compound.   (Central).

   b) The undermentioned equipment to be transferred from the Fireboat to the Launch.

      No. 2. Foam Branch and Knapsack Tank.
      Aircraft Rescue Gear Pack.
      Salvage Hook.
      Scramble Nets - 2
      Long Boat Hook.
      Aldis Lamp.
      Drift Axe.
      Felling Axe.
      First aid equipment (Gate House, Royal Pier).

   c) The crew will consist of a minimum of three men made up as follows:-

      1 Leading Fireman or above.
      1 Driver.
      1 Fireman,

      who will be required to man the Fire Appliances on the Auxiliary Launch.

      This Auxiliary Launch will not be equipped with wireless and all communication with it must be made through the Control Launch via Eastleigh Airport.

      E. T. HAYWARD.
      Chief Officer.

28th December, 1950.

Details of the fireboat cover provided at Southampton for Aquila Airways' flying boats as per Brigade Order No 81/1950.

Southampton Fire Brigade used this fireboat for safety cover in the 1950s. The Brigade later became part of Hampshire Fire Service. *Hampshire Fire Service*

should wear lifejackets. The firefighting equipment to be carried on board is also defined, as is the procedure to be followed in the event of having to use a launch from a local boatman. The fireboat would remain at the take-off position until the departing aircraft had flown beyond the point when it could return to Southampton if a problem had occurred.

The boat used in the 1950s was originally built for the National Fire Service in 1942 with the fleet number 290. When the NFS disbanded on 1 April 1948 it was transferred to Southampton where it was given the name *Fireboat 27*, the 27 merely being the fleet number. Known as an 'estuarial' class fireboat, it continued in service, crewed by personnel from the Docks Fire Station, until April 1963, when it was replaced by a new purpose-built fireboat. Originally it did not have a protected wheelhouse, although one was added during the 1950s. The fireboat was 53 feet long with a beam of 13 feet and a draught of 3ft 6in. It was fitted with four 700gpm pumps

The role played by the Fire Service may have only been a small one, but it was very important and has a rightful place in the heritage of marine aviation.

The magic of the swan

Royal Mail Airliner *Hampshire* was originally a 'Sunderland' flying boat built by Short Brothers at Belfast as works number JM 663, and was intended for war service with the RAF. However, it was acquired by BOAC on 12 November 1942 and registered G-AGEU as a civil 'Hythe' class flying boat for carrying freight and passengers, when it was given the name *Hampshire*.

Little else is known about this aircraft until it was bought by Aquila Airways in 1948, the change of ownership being recorded on 19 January 1949. The new owner purchased it in time to become the third Aquila aircraft used for the Berlin Airlift, although it only made six flights during this vast life-saving operation.

On 24 March 1949 *Hampshire* made the successful first flight from Southampton to Madeira, thus starting what became a regular route for the next nine years. This maiden flight was well reported in the press; a well-respected writer of the time, Mr Courtney Edwards, had a most interesting article concerning the event published in the aviation magazine *Flight* of 21 April 1949.

In 1950 *Hampshire* made another prestige flight, carrying Sir Winston Churchill as a passenger from Madeira to Southampton. By 1957, the last year for which passenger figures are available, the flying boat service carried

Summary of passengers travelling to and from Madeira by ship and Aquila Airways		
Year	Passengers disembarking and embarking	
	By ship	By Aquila
1949	19,370	1,528
1950	23,445	3,810
1951	25,145	5,122
1952	31,218	5,781
1953	35,948	5,380
1954	36,387	7,640
1955	34,825	8,730
1956	35,302	8,427
1957	35,552	11,927

almost a third of the total of tourists that visited Madeira.

Madeira had a long-established reputation for high-quality lace, embroidery, wickerwork and wine, as well as being an exclusive holiday resort, considered by many as a destination that is almost utopian! The island lies in the North Atlantic about 500km from the African coast and 1,000 km from mainland Portugal, and about half the population of around 260,000 live in the capital, Funchal. The idyllic island enjoys a mild climate thanks to the Gulf Stream and, although mountainous, boasts exotic vegetation in a wild profusion of colours, including wild orchids and bird of paradise flowers. The best way to 'discover' the

island is to visit it, and in the 1950s a new way was by a flying boat of Aquila Airways.

It was quite an exciting experience being a passenger aboard a flying boat when it took to the air. At first, as it gathered speed, the tail would drop into the water for a few seconds, which would rush by in a mass of foam. As the nose – or should it be the bow? – took to the air the whole aircraft would detach itself from one element, the sea, and become part of another, the air. Touching down, the pilot had no need to lower any landing gear – the very design of the flying boat made it natural to adapt from one element to the other with the grace of the swan. There was a swishing sound when the hull first made contact with the water, and it was not long before the flying boat was either safely moored to a buoy or, as at Southampton, snug in the U-shaped floating dock where disembarkation was by a gangway.

Southampton's reputation for handling large liners seems to have transferred itself to the handling of flying boat services, which lasted for a little over 20 years. In that time airline staff looked after tens of thousands of passengers and many tons of freight and mail, while of course the work put in by engineering staff made a sizeable contribution to this aspect of marine aviation history.

In August 1953 *Hampshire* was scrapped by Aquila after almost 11 years as a civil airliner.

A realistic model of 'Hythe' class flying boat *Hampshire* as it might have looked after the first flight to Madeira.

Wt 6327 6m/10/38 Wt & Sons Ltd 352/57093/24

NATIONALITY AND REGISTRATION

G-AGEU

FILE No. ____

DESCRIPTION OF AIRCRAFT Short S.25 "Sunderland" 3 then 5 Four-engined long-range Flying Boat

CONSTRUCTOR'S No. ____ JM 663

CERTIFICATE OF AIRWORTHINESS (if any). No. 6958

CERTIFICATE OF VALIDATION (if any). No. ____

CATEGORY ____ Normal

SUB-DIVISIONS ____ a, b, c, d, e.

Certificate No.	Full Name, Nationality and Address of Owner		Usual Station	Date of Registration	From the Date Shown, Registration Lapsed on Account of:—		
	Full Name and Address	Nationality			Change of Ownership of Aircraft	Destruction or Permanent Withdrawal from Use of Aircraft	Cancellation by the Secretary of State
9371/1	British Overseas Airways Corporation, Grand Spa Hotel, Clifton, Bristol 8.	British	Hythe	12.11.42	15.1.49.		
R.934/2	Aquila Airways Ltd., 5 Flights Avenue, London ... 6 Curzon Place, Park Lane, London W.	British		19.1.49.		18.8.53 Destroyed	

C.A. Form 113

The registration certificate for G-AGEU RMA *Hampshire*, which inaugurated Aquila Airways' Madeira service and also inspired first-flight passenger Constance Cumming to liken it to a swan. The certificate also records the aircraft's scrapping in August 1953.

Above A reminder of the past when draconian currency regulations were in force.

Below The very first passenger ticket issued by Aquila Airways, made out in the name of the company's founder and Managing Director Barry T. Aikman.

AQUILA AIRWAYS LIMITED

PASSENGER TICKET	SERIES NUMBER H Nº 00001

Place of Issue	Southampton	Date of Issue	23.3.49	Issued by

Name of Passenger	MR B.T Aikman

Place of Departure	S'ton	Agreed Stopping Place(s) (if any)	
Place of Destination	Madeira		Lisbon

Name and Address of Carrier
AQUILA AIRWAYS LIMITED,
5 Lloyds Avenue, Hamble,
London, E.C.3. Southampton.
Royal 5989. Hamble 3144

Remarks	
L of Embarkation 24/3/49	Charter, Fare Special Flight

FOR CONDITIONS OF CARRIAGE SEE BACK

Strike out if not applicable } ——— Liability limited under Rules of Warsaw Convention 1929

AQUILA AIRWAYS LIMITED

BAGGAGE CHECK (Luggage Ticket)	SERIES NUMBER H Nº 00001

Place of Departure	Southampton
Place of Destination	Madeira

Number of Pieces	2

Total Weight 25 kgs.	Free Allowance kgs.
	Excess Weight

Rate per kg.	Amount paid £ s. d.

For name and address of Carrier see Passenger Ticket

Place of Issue	S'ton	Date of Issue 24/3/49	Issued by

FOR CONDITIONS OF CARRIAGE SEE BACK

Strike out if not applicable } ——— Liability limited under Rules of Warsaw Convention 1929

Right Memories from modern-day Madeira: in the background of this Funchal waterfront scene is the P&O liner *Canberra* at her berth for a short visit to the island.

Left The entrance to the cathedral at Funchal; the building on the right was where Aquila Airways' handling agent was based.

Below A panoramic view of Funchal from the east. The harbour where the flying boats berthed can be clearly seen.

Right   Looking down on the fishing village of Camara de Lobos, where Sir Winston Churchill spent time painting. When Funchal could not be used by the flying boats this area afforded better sea conditions.

Below This is Machico, also once used as a diversion for the flying boats if sea conditions were bad at Funchal.

Left The flying boat 'swans' opened up access to Madeira by a route that bypassed the Bay of Biscay. Nowadays, with the land airfield, jets can reach the island from the UK in 3 hours, but thanks to Aquila Airways scenery like this was made available to the tourist in the 1950s.

The hovercraft

In the early 1950s Sir Christopher Cockerell carried out experiments to prove the feasibility of his theory about travelling on a cushion of air, and eventually this was to develop into the hovercraft. By all accounts he was a brilliant inventor, especially successful with his then employer, Marconi. However, at first he found it difficult to attract backers to support his work on the hovercraft, but after a while he approached the National Research & Development Corporation, which offered £1,000 subject to a gentlemen's agreement for a first refusal of any future developments. However, it was not until 1959 that commercial firms were licensed to develop the hovercraft, one such being Saunders Roe of Cowes, Isle of Wight.

The finance that became available in the 1960s resulted in Britain staying ahead in a project in which it had once enjoyed a

An advert from Vickers showing a car-carrying hovercraft that it was proposing for cross-Channel services.

Transport companies should be thinking in terms of Vickers Hovercraft

A Vickers car ferry operating from British shores in two years?

It is thoroughly practical to expect that in the near future Vickers Hovercraft will be running regular services for passengers, cars, and freight on waters around our shores. Terminals will be simple and easy to operate. The design of Vickers 150 ton craft shown here is finalised; it will travel at up to 75 knots. The ratio of cars to passengers carried will be adjusted to match the route. The most likely ratio will probably prove to be 24 cars to 200 passengers on routes of up to 100 miles. Alternatively, if no cars are carried, 600 passengers can be accommodated on routes of up to 50 miles. On such craft, people will travel smoothly and in comfort. They will drive their cars quickly and easily on board and disembark as easily. And their journey will take far, far less time. *Environmental experience with Vickers Hovercraft is greater than that of any other manufacturer in the world.*

Vickers have been carrying out project studies including very large craft with the ocean-going capability of conventional displacement vessels and able to travel at Hovercraft speeds. The Hovercraft Division is able to use Vickers vast shipbuilding experience.

VICKERS

VICKERS-ARMSTRONGS (ENGINEERS) LTD.
Itchen Works, Hazel Road,
Itchen, Southampton.

monopoly. By this time the Saunders Roe company had set up its hovercraft division and completed a prototype, known as the SR-N1, which crossed the Channel in 1959. Although behind the scenes there was controversy over costs, in the 1980s America paid the British Government over £3 million to be able to develop the hovercraft for military purposes.

Sir Christopher came to live in Hampshire, where he worked at Hythe, providing a strong link with local heritage, which was further strengthened when hovercraft began to operate on local passenger services from the mainland at Portsmouth to Ryde on the Isle of Wight. Indeed, larger versions were once operated on cross-Channel services carrying vehicles as well as passengers. Although renowned for speed, the service from Dover ceased to operate from October 2000.

It would appear that Sir Christopher did not gain great financial rewards from his invention, but his pioneering work was remembered when he was knighted in 1969. He died in 1999.

Princess too late

The superlatives should never be exhausted! She was the finest and ought to have been the aerial equivalent of Cunard's 'Queen' liners. However, in court circles a Princess is not allowed precedence over a Queen, and it certainly seemed as if this protocol ruled in passenger transport!

Undoubtedly the Saunders Roe 'Princess' flying boat, with its advanced fly-by-wire controls, was ahead of its time, and appeared to be the aircraft of the future when the Chief Test Pilot, Geoffrey Tyson, took to the air on 22 August 1952 for a 35-minute flight. The crew consisted of Tyson, R. B. Stratton, S. Ingle, W. S. Worner, J. S. Booth, S. Welford, H. New, G. Jones, H. Palmer, M. Mabey, A. Walker and R. J. Wraith. After this maiden flight there followed a series of test flights that even included an appearance at the prestigious Farnborough Air Show. These trials continued until June 1954, by which time over 90 hours had been flown, considerably surpassing the performance of Howard Hughes's mighty

The huge yet graceful Sanders Roe 'Princess' flying boat G-ALUN flying over Southampton Docks. Note the two decks and ten engines. *GKN Westland Aerospace*

prototype 'Spruce Goose' flying boat, which only flew for a few hundred yards.

The sheer size of the aircraft speaks for itself. It had a wingspan of 209ft 6in (floats down) or 219ft 6in (floats raised), the tailplane span was 77ft 2in, and the wing area was 1,103sq ft. It was 148 feet long, 24ft 3in high to the top of hull or 53ft 7in overall, and 16ft 8in in the beam, with a draught of 8 feet. The gross weight was 141 tons at take-off, and it had a range of 5,500 miles at a maximum speed of 395mph; the cruising speed was 360mph at 32,500 feet. All the controls were power-operated by universally jointed shafts in self-aligned bearings.

Thus back in the early 1950s Britain had a new flying boat capable of carrying around 200 passengers on two decks in fully pressurised accommodation – surely the world should have been its oyster! Sadly for marine aviation, Britain's national carrier and other world airlines had opted for land aircraft, needing

acres of concrete for runways and terminal facilities, while the flying boat required no more than an open stretch of water – fresh or salt, it made no difference. At ports like Southampton there were already dockside facilities that could handle hundreds of passengers at any one time. Furthermore there also existed a first-class rail link from the quay to Waterloo Station in London.

Despite these strong arguments for operating the 'Princess', opinion had turned against flying boats and the aircraft was never operated commercially. At one time Aquila Airways was reported to have offered £3 million for the three aircraft built by Saunders Roe, which had even registered them – G-ALUN, the flying prototype, and the two that did not take to the air, G-ALUO and G-ALUP.

5. PRESENT AND FUTURE, 1959 ONWARDS

Nostalgia preserved

It is fitting that there are still a few Short Brothers flying boats on show in museums around the world; that the total is only eight takes nothing away from the worldwide affection for this type of aircraft. In their heyday flying boats were built by several nations for military and civil use, and the fact that the 'Sunderland' was used by the air forces of other countries underlines the international regard that existed, and still exists, for marine aviation.

In reviewing the various flying boats on display in aviation museums, it is fitting to start at Southampton, where the Hall of Aviation, dedicated to R. J. Mitchell, is shortly to be relocated to Marchwood on the New Forest side of the River Test, where it will link up with the Powerboat Trust Restoration Group. Perhaps the main attraction at Southampton, albeit in the livery of Australia's Ansett Airways, is the 'Sandringham' flying boat. The visitor can walk on board the aircraft and savour the atmosphere of a bygone age, while there are, of course, further exhibits including

the Supermarine SR 6 and the 'Spitfire', together with others that are related to the local marine aviation heritage that should satisfy the discerning aviation 'buff'.

While the museum at Southampton is dedicated to the designer of the 'Spitfire', the other UK museums at Duxford and Hendon are more RAF-orientated, and both house versions of the wartime 'Sunderland' flying boat.

A short journey across the Channel, almost retracing the flight of Louis Bleriot back in 1909, takes us to Le Bourget, Paris, and another 'Sandringham'. This aircraft is in the livery of the French airline that operated it between the French-ruled islands in the Pacific

Below **Although several flying boats have been preserved, many of those made redundant by BOAC were scrapped, and here are some awaiting their fate at Hamworthy, Poole.** *Mrs Johnson*

Above right **Front cover of the brochure for the Hall of Aviation at Southampton.**

Right **Part of the passenger accommodation aboard the 'Sandringham' flying boat in the Southampton museum.**

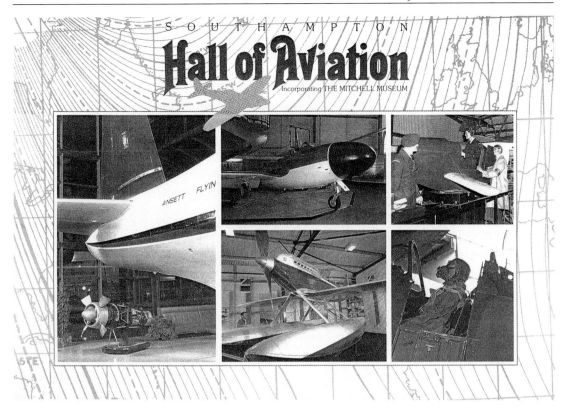

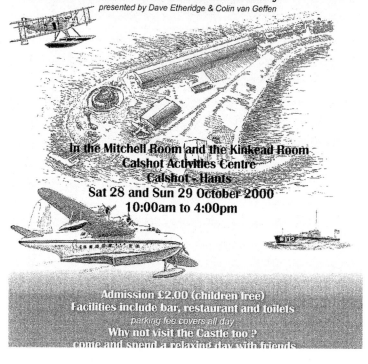

CALSHOT:
the Flying Years
an exhibition of photographs, postcards and illustrations depicting Calshot's connections with local aviation history
presented by Dave Etheridge & Colin van Geffen

In the Mitchell Room and the Kinkead Room
Calshot Activities Centre
Calshot - Hants
Sat 28 and Sun 29 October 2000
10:00am to 4:00pm

Admission £2.00 (children free)
Facilities include bar, restaurant and toilets
parking fee covers all day
Why not visit the Castle too ?
come and spend a relaxing day with friends

Left Into a new century and the interest goes on: a poster giving details of an event at the former RAF station at Calshot.

Below A present-day view of former Calshot station. The large hangar on the left is now an activity centre, while the tall tower houses the radar equipment that monitors shipping arriving at and leaving the Port of Southampton.

One of eight survivors worldwide, this is Duxford's 'Sunderland'.

Ocean, and it has an interesting history. It was built in 1944 as a 'Sunderland', and after the war was one of three converted to the 'Bermuda' class when its ownership changed from Short Brothers to BOAC, which registered it as G-AKCO and named it *St George*. It then saw service with BOAC until the national airline finished with flying boats in 1954, when Sir Gordon Taylor purchased it. Sir Gordon, perhaps better known as P. G. Taylor, was an aviation pioneer who planned to use the aircraft as an 'air yacht' on flights to exotic lagoons in the South Pacific; after all, he had already opened up such routes using a 'Catalina'.

When he acquired the flying boat it was overhauled at Cowes and a crew was recruited to fly it from the Solent to Australia. Two members of that crew were Christopher Blackburn, who later became a flight captain with Aquila Airways, and Douglas Hoyle, who was a radio operator with the same airline. The delivery flight started on 6 November 1954, and a leisurely pace was further slowed by a protracted delay at Malta due to adverse sea conditions. Eventually the aircraft reached Sydney and docked at the Rose Bay flying boat terminal.

At this stage Christopher Blackburn decided to go round the world and planned his first stop at Tahiti. When the time came for his departure, six weeks later, he took a last look at the 'Bermuda' that had brought him to

Australia, which by this time had been registered as VH-APG and renamed *Frigate Bird III*. He naturally thought that it would be the last time he would see this particular flying boat. He then received a telegram from Aquila Airways offering to employ him to fly a 'Solent' Mk IV from Auckland to the UK, so instead of visiting Tahiti he was on the flight deck of *Awatere* for the flight back to England. At 19 minutes past 2 on the afternoon of 5 February 1955 he was again in a flying boat on Southampton Water.

While his career with Aquila went from strength to strength the 'Bermuda' found another owner and, in 1958, a French registration, F-OBIP. At this time it was piloted by Commander Pearson, who flew it to and from French Polynesian islands with magical-sounding names like Bora-Bora. Commander Pearson's son was the senior pilot for Aquila and it was he who offered the flying boat to the museum at Le Bourget.

Some time in 1979 Christopher Blackburn visited Le Bourget with his wife and, after a gap of 24 years, saw again the flying boat he had once flown from Southampton, albeit now in French livery with its tailplane bearing the logo of RAI (Reseau Aerien Interinsulaire), the last company to operate the aircraft.

In the United States is Polk City, near Orlando, Florida, where Kermit Weekes has the 'living history' museum 'Fantasy of Flight' with many wartime aircraft including a

TOTALS Brought Forward: 5369:35 | 1494:10 | 1318:00 | 235:00 | 574:00

Date 1955	Type	Markings	Engines / Radio	Captain	Holder's Operating Capacity	From	To	Departure	Arrival	Day In Charge	Day Second	Night In Charge	Night Second	Instrument Flying	Remarks
13 JAN	SOLENT	ZK-AMN	4 HERCULES	Mc.GRANE	P₂	AUKLAND	LOCAL	0255	0440	1.45					INITIAL CIRCUITS & LANDINGS, DAY
13 "		MK IV	"	SELF	"	AUKLAND	LOCAL	0745	09.10		.25		1.00	.30	" " " NIGHT
19 "		"	"		P?	AUKLAND	LOCAL	0345	0545	2.00		1.00			AIR TEST & COMPASS SWING
25 "		GANYI	"		"	AUKLAND	SYDNEY	2333	0703	7.30					
26 "		"	"		"	SYDNEY	SYDNEY	1217	1312			:55		.30	R.T.B. GULPING No 3 ENGINE
27 "		"	"		"	SYDNEY	DARWIN	1059	2149	.45		10:05		.30	
28 "		"	"		"	DARWIN	SINGAPORE	2109	0754	10.45					
30 "		"	"		"	SINGAPORE	CHINA BAY	0340	1150	8.10					
31 "		"	"		"	CHINA BAY	KARACHI	0215	1010	7.55					
										37.05	2.10	11.20	1.00		

TOTALS Carried Forward: 5406:40 | 1496:20 | 1329:30 | 236:00 | 575:30

8468 : 00

TOTALS Brought Forward: 5406:40 | 1496:20 | 1329:00 | 236:00 | 575:30

Date 1955	Type	Markings	Engines / Radio	Captain	Holder's Operating Capacity	From	To	Departure	Arrival	Day In Charge	Day Second	Night In Charge	Night Second	Instrument Flying	Remarks
1 FEB	SOLENT	GANYI	4 HERCULES	SELF	P₁	KARACHI	BAHREIN	0408	1228	6.20					PRELIMINARY PROVING FLIGHT.
2 "		MK IV	"		"	BAHREIN	FANARA	0549	1304	7.15					FOR GENOA SERVICE.
3 "		"	"		"	FANARA	GENOA	0430	1415	9.45					
5 "		"	"		"	GENOA	SOUTHAMPTON	0939	1419	5.40					
19 "		SOLENT	GANAT	"		"	SOUTHAMPTON	LISBON	0212	0842	1.30		5.00		.30	40 PAX
19 "		MKIII	("	"		"	LISBON	MADEIRA	1005	1425	4.20					40 "
24 "		"	GAKNU	"		"	MADEIRA	LISBON	1115	1450	3.35					42 "
25 "		"	"	"		"	LISBON	SOUTHAMPTON	0815	1410	5.55				.30	31 " QDM LET-DOWN.
										44.20					

TOTALS Carried Forward: 5451:00 | 1496:20 | 1334:00 | 236:00 | 576:30

8517 : 20

Extracts from Captain Evans's flight logbook for the delivery flight of the 'Solent' Mk IV from Auckland to Southampton between 13 January and 5 February 1955. Twenty-four years later Christopher Blackburn saw her again in the museum in Le Bourget.

'Sunderland' flying boat that once operated, in tandem, with the aircraft in the museum at Southampton. Before its purchase by Mr Weekes it was owned by Edward Hulton, of the *Picture Post* family, while a anther interesting previous owner was Captain Charles Blair, who also owned Antilles Airboats and was married to Maureen O'Hara, the American film star.

On the USA's Pacific coast there is yet another British-built flying boat, this time a 'Solent' at the Western Aerospace Museum at Oakland, San Francisco. Once owned by Trans Oceanic Airways, which intended to operate it from the USA and connect with cruise liners in the Pacific, this flying boat was purchased by Howard Hughes before being acquired by the present owners and placed on display at Oakland.

On the other side of the world, a visit can to be made to the Museum of Transport and Technology (MOTAT) at the Sir Keith Park Memorial Airfield Hangar at Auckland, New Zealand. There a wartime 'Sunderland', as operated by the Royal New Zealand Air Force, is on show adjacent to a fully refurbished 'Solent' Mk IV flying boat. The latter is similar to the two purchased by Aquila Airways from TEAL and ferried from New Zealand to England back in 1955.

In addition to the museums mentioned, flying boat memorabilia can also be seen at

Above A leaflet describing the 'Fantasy of Flight' attraction at Polk City, Florida, USA, where the flying boat once owned by Edward Hulton is a major exhibit.

Below **The 'Fantasy of Flight' aircraft shortly before it left Southampton to fly to Polk City.** *Ken Carmichael*

ABOUT THE MUSEUM

You'll experience the romance of a bygone era aboard the Western Aerospace Museum's Flying Boat, shown here at the Honolulu Airport in 1954.

Background

The Western Aerospace Museum (WAM) is a non-profit institution. In 1988 we acquired our current exhibition space.

Since opening our doors to the public, we have generated a significant increase in volunteer participation and corporate involvement; undergone major renovations and successfully implemented an aggressive acquisitions program.

Historic location and expanding facilities

The Museum's facilities are located in a vintage hangar at Oakland International Airport's historic North Field. This hangar, an educational center and administration building, a restoration shop, and an outdoor exhibition area are provided by the Port of Oakland. The hangar, now full of historic aircraft, was built in 1940 by the Boeing School of Aeronautics and was used to train aircraft mechanics for the U.S. Army Air Corps and Navy during World War II.

The Flying Boat

Our most spectacular exhibit is the Short Solent 4-engine Flying Boat. She was built in 1946 as an upgraded version of the famous World War II British Sunderland. She measures almost 90 feet long, with the tip of her tail 37 feet above the ground. She is designed to take off and land in the water only.

In 1949 the Flying Boat was converted for luxury passenger transport service, carrying up to 39 passengers in comfortable splendor. She flew such exotic routes as England to South Africa for British Overseas Airways Corporation, and in Australia for Trans Oceanic Airways.

In 1957 she and two sister ships were purchased by South Pacific Air Lines for service between Honolulu and Tahiti. They were flown to Alameda, California, to be rebuilt to comply with U.S. regulations. In 1959, when the project was cancelled due to nuclear testing on Christmas Island (the proposed refueling stop), the ships were sold to Howard Hughes.

After the death of Howard Hughes, two of the Flying Boats were broken up for scrap, but the last one was rescued in 1976 by the current owners, Rick and Randy Grant, who have dedicated themselves to restoring her to operational status. She has been on display at North Field since 1987.

Other exhibits in our collection

In addition to the Flying Boat, the Museum offers many other exhibits, including a fully-

functioning post-WWII Link instrument trainer. Visitors can also view an airplane similar to the one Amelia Earhart was flying when she disappeared over the Pacific Ocean after taking off from North Field in 1937. She was undertaking a journey that would have made her the first woman to fly around the world. The Western Aerospace Museum boasts a growing collection of noteworthy aircraft and engines.

Amelia Earhart in the cockpit of her L-10. Photo by Albert L. Bresnick, 1937

Other exhibits include Early Oakland Aviation, African-American Aviation, Women Pilots, Jimmy Doolittle/The 8th Air Force, Gold

Left Details of the Western Aerospace Museum at Oakland, California, home of a 'Solent' flying boat.

Below 'Solent' *City of Cardiff* at the Oakland museum, with former Aquila Flight Engineer Don Townend propping up the bow. *Don Townend*

Short S45A Solent Mark 4 Flying Boat
ZK-AMO "Aranui"*
*(Maori for "MAIN PATHWAY")

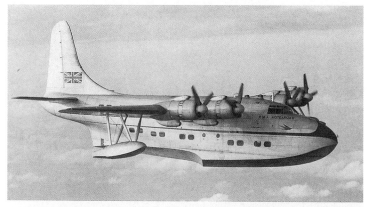

FOYNES
The Centre of
the Aviation World
1939-1945

The only surviving Mark 4 Solent in the world.

The four Mk.4 Short Solent Flying Boats supplied to Tasman
Empire Airways Ltd., were named and registered:

- AOTEAROA II ZK-AML
- ARARANGI ZK-AMM
- AWATERE ZK-AMN
- ARANUI ZK-AMO

The Solent Flying Boats operated successfully and safely from 1949
until 1954 when all the services were taken over by landplanes using
Douglas DC 6's. However, the Suva to Papeete route remained the
preserve of the Flying Boat and it was not until September 1960 that
the last service was operated by ZK-AMO, the aircraft now in the
Museum of Transport & Technology (M.O.T.A.T.), Auckland.

This aircraft is the last big Flying Boat built specifically as a civilian
airliner to go into regular passenger service.

*Refurbishing the aircraft has been undertaken by the Solent Flying Boat
Preservation Society, members of whom wish to preserve a piece of
New Zealand's international aviation history for future generations.*

Left A leaflet from the Museum of
Transport and Technology at
Auckland, New Zealand, where
there is a 'Sunderland' as well as
this 'Solent' Mk IV flying boat.

Above A leaflet from Foynes Flying
Boat Museum in Co Limerick,
Irish Republic. For many years
Foynes was an international flying
boat base, especially so during the
Second World War. Now air traffic
is handled at nearby Shannon
Airport.

smaller establishments, such as at Foynes, in
the Irish Republic, Poole in Dorset, and Oban
in Scotland. Although the Foynes Flying Boat
Museum does not exhibit a flying boat, its
interest lies in the fact that it is housed in what
was accommodation formerly used for cargo
and passenger handling. Even the original air
traffic control tower is part of a museum now
dedicated to displaying memorabilia
associated with marine aviation 50 or so years
ago. The past importance of Foynes was
emphasised when the opening ceremony was
performed by film actress Maureen O'Hara,
whose late husband, the abovementioned
Captain Charles Blair, enjoyed a long
association with Foynes; this was no doubt a

factor in her support of the museum, which
opened on the 50th anniversary of the first
scheduled Pan American flying boat flight
from New York to Foynes on 8 July 1939. That
day had another significance in 1976 when
Miss O'Hara and Captain Blair flew the
Atlantic in *Southern Cross*, the flying boat that
is now on display at the Aviation Museum in
Southampton. Also, as mentioned earlier in
this book, about 60 years ago the River
Shannon at Foynes was a terminal for flying
boats operated by American Export Airlines,
Imperial Airways (later to become BOAC).
and Pan American Airways, and many
thousands of passengers enjoyed the warm
welcome that made Foynes so popular.

Above **Pan American Boeing 314 *Yankee Clipper* at Foynes in the days when it was an international flying boat base.** *Foynes Flying Boat Museum*

Below **Excalibur, a Sikorsky VS 44 of American Export. These flying boats were flown by Captain Charles Blair; he was married to actress Maureen O'Hara, who opened the Foynes Flying Boat Museum in July 1989.** *Foynes Flying Boat Museum*

Sea Wings 2000

This was the name given to a Millennium celebration held in Southampton over the weekend of 3-4 June 2000. There was some question as to whether the flying display should take place, since an unfortunate accident had occurred on 27 July 1998 when a 'Catalina' amphibian taking part in an advance publicity demonstration had plunged into Southampton Water on take-off. Although there were survivors, the then Mayor of the City of Southampton and an employee of an airline at Southampton Airport lost their lives.

Naturally the first reaction was to cancel the entire project because of the sad memories that might have been evoked by the aviation spectacular. However, the celebration went ahead more or less as originally planned. It was not only a fitting tribute to the victims of the earlier tragedy, but also celebrated the involvement of Southampton in the field of marine aviation over several decades. As can be judged from the flying programme, tributes were paid to a range of local aviation achievements that included the Supermarine 'Spitfire', especially when, on the day, no fewer than 13 'Spits' took to the air and flew in formation over Southampton Water.

The Sea Wings spectacular proved to be a most worthy successor to an event staged by Southampton City Council to mark the 60th Anniversary of the 'Spitfire' back in 1996. The Millennium programme was longer, being an all-day event and considered by many to have been much more marine-orientated, as there were several interesting aircraft such as the Grumman 'Albatross' and 'Goose', the Piaggio 'Royal Gull' and the De Havilland 'Beaver', all

of which were as happy on the water as in the air. Supporting displays included air-sea rescue demonstrations and, for land aircraft enthusiasts, there were the 'Spitfires', the Hawker 'Hurricane' and the Fairey 'Swordfish'.

Certainly these marine aircraft helped to make it a day that will be remembered by many people for years to come, and although Sea Wings 2000 effectively closed a century of marine aviation, it would be nice to think that a new project will herald the start of another century of flying boats...

Finale

Just when it seems that flying boats have been consigned to history, it is exciting to hear and read of the aspirations of James Labouchere at Warrior (Aero-Marine) Limited, Lymington, Hampshire. Here is a man surely following the footsteps of Sam Saunders, A. V. Roe and Scott-Paine with a projected flying boat called the 'Centaur'. As can be seen from the brochure, this aircraft brings to the early 21st century a modernised version of some of the earlier designs such as the Supermarine 'Walrus' manufactured by Saunders Roe during the Second World War.

The 'Centaur' is truly an amazing aircraft that will be able to shorten the time taken travelling from one marina to another, and the folding wings mean that it can even be moored alongside the holiday yacht. Its versatility does not end there, however, as being amphibian it is also capable of operation from a land airfield, while its seagoing attributes could see the 'Centaur' used as a 'flying yacht'. This exciting project has recently been the recipient of the top 'Smart Exceptional Award' for 2001, bringing a cheque for £450,000.

It is heart-warming to know that the spirit of bygone entrepreneurs, some already mentioned, is going to be rekindled in this century with James Labouchere's aircraft. It would be even nicer to think that if a second flying boat were to be designed, its name might be 'Aquila'.

Which brings us back to Aquila Airways. In 1951 the newly married Margaret and Dennis Thatcher, flying to Madeira on board an

Aquila flying boat, did not receive the media attention that would become routine when she became Prime Minister, but 50 years later Baroness Thatcher and her husband returned to Madeira and stayed at the same hotel, The Savoy. On 18 November 2001 the *Mail on Sunday* published a romantic story about the couple and their sentimental journey, and its author, Suzanna Chambers, followed it up a week later with a story about Aquila Airways, Britain's last all-flying boat airline. If this young lady and her newspaper's readers are showing such an interest in a bygone age of air travel, then perhaps marine aviation 'nutters' like myself should not have any worries for the future of the 'Centaur' project.

Warrior (Aero-Marine) Ltd is a new aerospace company which is developing the "CENTAUR" to unleash the full potential of the amphibious aircraft concept.

The Centaur is for services, business, private utility and recreation. It is competitive with much of the equivalent landplane fleet. It offers fundamental new benefits over equivalent seaplanes.

high load capacity and payload-range is achieved with the new low-drag hull and a high-lift aerodynamic configuration.

easy loading on land or water with large doors and a utility/loading platform providing by the broad stub-wings.

access to about five times as many coastal facilities is enabled by the use of a conventional folding wing.

operation in 80 percent larger waves is made acceptable by the hull's new features including fine bow, without transverse step or forebody chines.

low maintenance and a long structural life in salt-water is achieved with the extensive use of composites.

These advantages overcome the major limitations of seaplanes. The Centaur opens doors to greater competitiveness in existing seaplane applications and to a wide range of new destinations, new operations and new aviation practices.

Warrior (Aero-Marine) Ltd's 'Centaur' amphibious aircraft, being developed beside the Solent at Lymington, Hampshire: a new chapter in the flying boat story?

APPENDIX:
MARINE AVIATION BUSINESSES OF THE SOLENT AREA

This list includes not only the businesses mentioned in this book, but also others involved with marine aviation in the South, some of which came to prominence during the 1939-45 war as sub-contractors. However, most that are listed were in fact involved in original development.

Isle of Wight
J. Samuel White
S. E. Saunders; later became known as Saunders Roe and more recently GKN Westland Aerospace

Mainland
Beardmore Engines
British Power Boat Co
Camper & Nicholson
Cunliffe Owen
Curtiss; the local sole concessionaire was Captain E. Bass c/o Luke & Co of Hamble
Fairey Aviation
Folland Aircraft Co
Hubert Scott-Paine
Luke & Co
McCardle & Drexel
Eric Moon; set up an engineering works in 1910 at the historic war house in Southampton
May, Hardern & May

Pemberton Billing
A. V. Roe
Sopwith Aviation
Supermarine
Vickers Armstrong

Airlines
Aquila Airways Limited
BOAC
British Marine Air Navigation; operated daily services from Woolston, Southampton, to St Peter Port, Guernsey, with Supermarine 'Sea Eagle'
Imperial Airways
Pan American Airways

INDEX